Immigrant American Women Role Models

Immigrant American Women Role Models

Fifteen Inspiring Biographies, 1850–1950

by
Moira Davison Reynolds

McFarland & Company, Inc., Publishers
Jefferson, North Carolina, and London

To Ron and Diana
and their children,
Brittany, Drew and Avery,
with love

British Library Cataloguing-in-Publication data are available

Library of Congress Cataloguing-in-Publication Data

Reynolds, Moira Davison.
    Immigrant American women role models : fifteen inspiring
biographies, 1850–1950 / by Moira Davison Reynolds.
       p. cm.
    Includes index.
    ISBN 0-7864-0409-4 (library binding : 55# alkaline paper) ∞
    1. Women immigrants — United States — Biography.   2. Role models —
United States — Biography. I. Title.
HQ1412.D38   1997
305.48'9691 — dc21
                                                97-34100
                                                     CIP

Manufactured in the United States of America

*McFarland & Company, Inc., Publishers
  Box 611, Jefferson, North Carolina 28640*

Contents

Illustrations

Preface and Acknowledgments

The women in this book are immigrants to the United States who made significant contributions during the period 1850–1950. I selected them more on the basis of my own interest than on their national origins. The book is aimed at the general reader interested in United States history, not at the professional historian. It should have particular appeal to women.

My thanks are due to Sister Mary Louise Sullivan for suggestions on the chapter on Mother Cabrini; to Barbara Patrick for reviewing the chapter on Senda Berenson; and to Vivian Lasich for critical reading of the chapter on Eva Le Gallienne.

I am indebted to several institutions for providing helpful information: Hobart-Smith College, Warren Hunting Smith Library; New York University, Elmer Holmes Bolst Library; Smith College Archives; Radcliffe College, Schlesinger Library; University of Wisconsin Archives; Ohio Historical Society; Cincinnati Art Museum; Catholic Health Partners; The Salvation Army Archives and Research Center; National League for Nursing, New York Downtown Hospital; UNITE!; and the Helena Rubinstein Foundation.

I am grateful to members of the staffs of Peter White Public Library in Marquette and Lydia M. Olson Library of Northern Michigan University for their cooperation. I once again express my admiration for Joanne Whitley of Superiorland Library Cooperative, who continues to locate hard-to-find materials.

Moira Davison Reynolds
Marquette, Michigan

Introduction

*Often, people don't try to accomplish some-
thing because they aren't capable of it. But
just as often, people aren't capable of accomplishing something because they aren't trying.*
Marilyn vos Savant
Parade Magazine— June 9, 1996

The years 1850–1950 reflect great progress in women's rights. As of the mid-nineteenth century, American women were not permitted to vote or hold public office. Many states allowed husbands to beat their wives "with a reasonable instrument." Wives' earnings legally belonged to their husbands, and married women could not hold property in their own names. In divorce cases, husbands rather than wives were very likely to be given custody of children. A wife could not file a lawsuit or be sued. Wives received the same legal treatment as children or adults who were insane or mentally retarded. The lot of a single woman was only slightly better. For married and single alike, there were cultural restrictions; for example, women did not speak before mixed audiences, and they did not enter professions such as law, medicine or the divinity. By 1950, these restrictions had disappeared and there was significant progress towards equality of the sexes.

The period studied in this work includes decisive events in the history of the United States. In the nineteenth century, the nation's unity was tested by a devastating civil war; in the twentieth, the nation emerged from two exhausting world wars as the leading power. It was a nation blessed with immense natural resources and hardy people. Among these people — of many races, religions and cultures — were many immigrants and their descendants.

Since the years under consideration herein reflect the enormous

1

contribution of European immigrants, this book is the story of 15 women of European descent who made their mark on the culture of their adopted country.

British-born Elizabeth Blackwell became, in 1849, after concentrated effort, the first woman to graduate from an American medical college. Eight years later, with two other female physicians, she opened the New York Infirmary for Women and Children. In conjunction with the Infirmary, Elizabeth and her sister Emily founded a medical college for women that operated for 31 years. The barriers against women in medicine were gradually broken down; by 1950, woman physicians, although not numerous, were familiar to the American public.

The same year that Elizabeth Blackwell graduated from medical school, Lilly Martin Spencer, the British-born daughter of French parents, became known in the United States as a painter. At an exhibit in 1852, her works sold for more than those of John Audubon. In 1869, she completed her *Truth Unveiling Falsehood*. It was exhibited at the Centennial Exhibition in Philadelphia in 1876.

In Germany, Friederich Froebel devoted much of his life to the education of young children. Maria Kraus-Boelté brought his methods to the United States with the opening of the New York Seminary for Kindergartners. In time the school not only taught thousands of children, but also trained hundreds of conventional Froebelian teachers.

Anna Howard Shaw, of English birth, preached in pioneer settlements and lumber camps, sometimes carrying a revolver to protect herself. In 1878, she graduated from Boston University's School of Theology, and in 1880, the Methodist Protestant Church granted her ordination after more mainstream Methodistism had refused it and also revoked her license to preach. Graduating in medicine in 1886, she had a long career as an advocate for temperance and woman suffrage.

In 1998, Mother Cabrini arrived in New York City to aid poor Italians in the land to which they had immigrated. For some 25 years she founded convents, schools, orphanages and hospitals.

Mary Adelaide Nutting, Canadian by birth, graduated in 1891 from Johns Hopkins Hospital School for Nurses, a member of its first class. Her life work was to make nursing a true profession. In 1910, she became head of the new department of nursing and health at Teachers College, Columbia University.

Born in what was then Austria, Ernestine Schumann-Heink made her debut with the Metropolitan Opera Company in 1889. Noted for her Wagnerian roles, she was considered the world's leading contralto of her day.

Another religious person dedicated to social welfare was London-born Evangeline Cory Booth. In 1904, she became commander of the Salvation Army in the United States. She instituted hospitals for unwed mothers and homes for working women and for the aged. During World War I, her organization of canteens for soldiers in France, along with the presence of caring Salvationists, prompted a new respect for the Salvation Army. She was responsible for introducing improved fundraising methods.

Senda Berenson, born in Lithuania, advanced women's sports. While an athletic instructor at Smith College, she introduced women's basketball, which modified the rules of the men's game. She edited the official rules from 1899 to 1917, with her version remaining the standard for 70 years.

In 1914, an enterprising Polish entrepreneur named Helena Rubinstein opened a beauty salon in New York City. By the time of her death in 1965, her beauty products were widely known and she had developed a multimillion dollar business.

Russian-born Sophie Simon Loeb used her journalistic ability to bring about social reform. Her special areas of concern were widowed mothers and child welfare. Appointed to New York City's Child Welfare Board in 1915, she became its president and later made it into a model organization. Her reform interests were many and varied — she once mediated a New York City taxi strike.

A stage actress from Canada named Gladys Smith took the name of Mary Pickford. By 1914, her success in silent movies had given her the title of "America's Sweetheart." Her first talking picture brought her a 1929 Academy Award for Best Actress.

Working conditions in the garment industry engaged the energy of Dorothy Jacobs Bellanca, who came to the United States from Latvia. By the age of 13, she was working as a hand buttonhole maker in a clothing factory. Around 1909, she helped form Local 170 of the United Garment Workers of America and later led this local union into the more radical Amalgamated Clothing Workers of America. She worked tirelessly to gain equality for women in union matters.

Some women were attracted to science, among them Gerty Cori, originally from Prague. In 1920, she obtained a medical degree there, and two years later, moved with her husband, Carl Cori, to Buffalo, New York, to do medical research. Their work ultimately centered on the metabolism of glycogen, for which they shared the 1947 Nobel Prize with Barnardo Houssay of Argentina. Naturalized in 1928, Gerti Cori thus became the first American woman to receive a Nobel Prize in science.

An actress and director of note was Eva Le Gallienne. Educated in London, her birthplace, and in Paris, she made her debut in New York City in 1915. Between 1926 and 1932, her Civic Repertory Theatre gave 1,581 performances of 34 different plays, most of which she both starred in and directed. She came to be known as an outstanding interpreter of Ibsen.

The contributions of these 15 women vary considerably in consequence, yet each is worthy of notice. Collectively they assisted the advancement of women and individually added some firsts to the history of these immigrants' chosen country.

Elizabeth Blackwell

"If I could have been treated by a lady doctor, my worst suffering would have been spared me." A dying woman voiced this sentiment to 24-year-old Elizabeth Blackwell in 1845.

The idea of a lady doctor was so foreign to the thinking of the day that Miss Blackwell at once repudiated the suggestion as an impossible one. But the thought of a woman physician administering to women kept recurring and eventually spurred her to pursue a career in medicine.

Elizabeth Blackwell was born February 3, 1821, in the port city of Bristol, England. Her mother was Hannah (Lane) Blackwell, a woman noted for her steadfast devotion to religion. Her father, Samuel Blackwell, owned a sugar refinery. A dissenter from the established Church of England, he, like his wife, was religious. He was also an advocate of reform in politics. He had liberal ideas, including the belief that girls should be as well educated as boys. The couple had 13 children, nine of whom survived. Elizabeth, known to her family as Bessie, was the third daughter. She would not be the only child with progressive ideas: her sister Emily would follow her into medicine; one brother would marry Lucy Stone, the eminent feminist; and another brother would take as his wife Antoinette Brown, among the first women in the United States to be ordained as a minister. *Those Extraordinary Blackwells*, a 1967 book by Elinor Rice Hays, presents the idiosyncrasies of the family as well as its strengths. It emphasizes the strong family ties.

The Blackwell household included some unmarried female relatives who influenced Elizabeth's upbringing. Religion was a part of her life from childhood and remained so, but she did not have the pious attitude of her mother. The family lived in comfort — for example, Elizabeth had governesses. Her autobiography was written in old age and possibly not reliably because of the time span. In it she described her home life as "rich and satisfying"; some of her siblings were less enthusiastic about their childhood.

When she was 11, the family moved to the United States, mainly because of reverses in Samuel's business. This was a major uprooting, especially painful to Hannah. But women of her day were accustomed to follow their men without protest. In August 1832, the family party of eight children (plus one en route), father, mother, three aunts, governess and two servants left Bristol on the sailing ship *Cosmos*, bound for New York. There were 200 passengers and the voyage took a little longer than seven weeks. A cow, brought aboard as a source of milk, soon died. More serious were several deaths among the steerage passengers. According to Elizabeth's recollections, they died of cholera. The Blackwells were spared, suffering only from seasickness.

With his strong social conscience, Samuel Blackwell hoped to find improved conditions in America. Ironically, slavery still existed in the so-called land of the free after the practice had been outlawed in 1772 in the land of his birth. The ruling did not, however, apply to British possessions. Samuel's great hero, William Wilburforce, had helped to bring about the British Bill of Abolition, stipulating that as from January 1, 1797, "all manner of dealing and trading in the purchase or transfer of slaves, or of persons intending to be sold in, at, or from any part of the continent or countries of Africa" was to be "utterly abolished, prohibited, and declared to be unlawful." The act was not as effective as intended, but it was a beginning. On August 9, 1833, Parliament did free all slaves in the British colonies.

The fact that his sugar business was supported by slave labor had always bothered Samuel. He had high hopes that now he could use beets as a source of sugar, and thus avoid buying from Cuban planters. The children were well aware of their father's antislavery attitude, and it is not surprising that some of them remember William Lloyd Garrison as a welcome visitor to their new-world home.

The Blackwells lived at first in Jersey City. During this time, Elizabeth attended school in New York City, taking a ferryboat across the bay. The family later lived in a country house on Long Island.

In 1838, they moved to Cincinnati because the business was not prospering. The trip took nine days, involving travel by train and canal boat and then sailing down the Ohio River. Samuel died within a few months of their arrival, leaving Hannah and his nine children with very little income.

To support the family, the three oldest girls started a day and boarding school for young ladies, and the oldest son found a position. The school was abandoned after about four years, at which time the other brothers were able to find employment.

In Cincinnati, Elizabeth seems to have been influenced by William Henry Channing, a Unitarian minister and nephew of the famous William Ellery Channing of Boston. It was probably through him that she learned to appreciate Emerson, Thoreau, Margaret Fuller and others.

After having private pupils for a brief stint, Elizabeth went to teach at a newly established district school in rural Henderson, located in western Kentucky. She stayed only one term, because, according to her autobiography, a slave state caused continual outrage to her sense of justice.

It was after she had returned to her family that her dying friend's suggestion to study medicine received serious consideration. At 24 — her age — most women were married and had children. According to Blackwell's own writings, "whenever I became sufficiently intimate with any individual to be able to realize what a life association might mean, I shrank from the prospect, disappointed or repelled." She also noted that she was now determined to become a physician, "and thus place a strong barrier between me and all ordinary marriage. I must have something to engross my thoughts, some object in life." Biographers have noted that Blackwell was shy. This characteristic may have made it difficult for her to become acquainted with men, but it is not likely that this was the sole reason for her decision not to marry. It is noteworthy that each of the five Blackwell sisters in Elizabeth's immediate family remained single, as did three Blackwell aunts.

Blackwell reasoned that if her plan to enter medicine was worthy, she should be able to realize it. "The idea of winning a doctor's degree gradually assumed the aspect of a great moral crusade," she wrote. Apparently at that time, "female physician" meant an abortionist, exemplified by Ann Lohman — known as Madame Restell — who had become rich and famous by terminating pregnancies. Blackwell believed that applying the term to "those women who carried on this shocking trade" was a horror. "It was an utter degradation of what might and should become a noble position of women." She intended to represent a vastly different service to women. Such was the basis of her crusade.

Faced with an absence of role models to advise her about a woman becoming a physician, Blackwell solicited the opinions of a variety of persons. One of these was her neighbor in the Walnut Hills section of

Cincinnati, Harriet Beecher Stowe, later to become world famous as the author of *Uncle Tom's Cabin*. To Blackwell's disappointment, Harriet and Calvin Stowe considered the idea impractical to implement, but, they admitted, highly useful. Although she received little encouragement from others, Blackwell drew up a plan. Realizing she would need reserve finances, she decided to teach long enough to save what seemed sufficient.

Despite her dislike of slavery, she accepted a position as a music teacher in Asheville, North Carolina. Two brothers escorted her on the 11-day journey, since it was a custom for women not to travel alone. She had chosen the Asheville situation because she was an accomplished musician and because the principal, the Rev. John Dickson, had once been a doctor, and he consented to allow her to use his medical books. She lived with the Dicksons, who were kind to her.

To her consternation, she found that state law forbade her teaching slaves to read or write. She then organized a Sunday School "to teach them a religion which the owners professed to follow whilst violating its very first principles." A letter to her mother, dated July 1845, stated that as she looked round the little room and saw ladies holding forth to their slaves, convinced that they were model mistresses. She wanted to take the chains off slaves and "fasten them on their tyrants till they learned in dismal wretchedness the bitterness of that bondage they inflict." Then she added, "But one person can do nothing."

The Asheville school closed in 1846. (This was not unusual; most schools of that era had short lives.) Dr. John Dickson had a brother, Dr. Sam Dickson, who was a professor at the Medical College of Charleston, and the latter agreed to help Blackwell with her medical studies. This was important, because at the time, the apprenticeship method was still recognized in the instruction of medical students. She was invited to live with his family and they soon found her a teaching position. She found life in Charleston pleasant, recording such events as hearing an oration on states' rights by the eloquent John C. Calhoun and visiting a banana plantation.

Blackwell had continued to write letters to doctors, educators and progressive women for advice about her future. Emma Willard, who founded Troy Female Seminary, suggested she get the opinion of Dr. Joseph Warrington of Philadelphia, a Quaker.

Dr. Warrington thought that women were more suited to nursing the sick, but he invited her to confer with him if she came to Philadelphia. In the summer of 1847, Blackwell sailed from Charleston to

Philadelphia, then a center of American medicine. Apparently she was unescorted on this voyage; her diary entry noted that she took the ship to save money. She found lodgings with the family of Dr. William Elder and arranged for private lessons in anatomy. Dr. Warrington gave her advice and wrote recommendations on her behalf.

The four medical colleges of the city turned Blackwell down as a regular student. Two doctors suggested that she study in Paris — disguised as a male. After applications to established schools in other cities met with the same fate, she tried several smaller schools in northern states. All told, her rejections totaled 17.

Heartening news arrived from Geneva, New York. The dean of the faculty of Geneva College had enclosed an interesting document, a copy of which follows:

> At a meeting of the entire class of Geneva Medical College, held this day, October 20, 1847, the following resolutions were unanimously adopted: —
>
> 1. Resolved — *That one of the principles of a Republican Government is the universal education of both sexes; that to every branch of scientific education the door should be open equally to all; that the application of Elizabeth Blackwell to become a member of our class meets our entire approbation; and in extending our unanimous invitation we pledge ourselves that no conduct of ours shall cause her to regret her attendance at this institution.*
>
> 2. Resolved — *That a copy of these proceedings be signed by the chairman and transmitted to Elizabeth Blackwell.*
>
> T.H. Stratton, Chairman

She left Philadelphia, arriving in Geneva on November 6, 1847, to enroll as student number 130 in the medical department. The term had already begun, but she found a comfortable boarding house that was just a three-minute walk from the college.

Blackwell has been described at this time as a woman of small stature. She had long slender fingers which she hoped would be of benefit when she realized her goal of becoming a surgeon. Her eyes were gray-blue and her fair hair had acquired a reddish tinge. She dressed plainly and conducted herself with great dignity. Apparently the townspeople of Geneva were most curious about a would-be female doctor; she considered some of the women unfriendly.

The curriculum required three years' study under the supervision of a physician and attendance at two 16-week sessions at the college. Then there were examinations to be passed. The material given in the first session was repeated in the second without presentation of additional material.

That curriculum was obviously a far cry from today's rigorous requirements. Knowledge was scant — to illustrate, the science of microbiology was unknown, making surgery so risky that its application was very limited. In addition, a very serious weakness was the lack of clinical training. However, the practice of medicine was becoming more scientific and would soon advance significantly with the acceptance of the germ theory of disease.

The professor of anatomy, Dr. John Webster, was popular with the students, including Blackwell. When he requested her to excuse herself from dissection of the reproductive system, she wrote him a short note of protest. He agreed to permit her to be present. She wrote in her diary that the demonstration was just as much as she could bear. According to her, "Some of the students blushed, some were hysterical, not one could keep in a smile…. My delicacy was certainly shocked." Later Dr. Webster read her note, which stated that her purpose was serious and that she did not wish to miss lectures; however, if it were the desire of the class, she would stay away. The students indicated that they wholeheartedly approved of her presence.

A December entry in Blackwell's diary noted that she had been called to Dr. Webster's rooms when an indigent woman was being examined. "'Twas a horrible exposure; indecent for any poor woman to be subjected to such a torture…. I felt more than ever the necessity of my mission."

An article reprinted from the *Buffalo Medical Journal* appeared in the *Geneva Courier* of February 9, 1848. It made clear that as the term advanced, Blackwell was still welcome:

> Nothing has transpired as yet to disprove the action taken by the faculty and the class. In so far as her presence in the lecture room has had any influence, it has been conducive to more strict decorum than is usual with medical classes, and any embarrassment which may be felt by all parties has long since disappeared.

When the first session ended late in January, Blackwell returned to Philadelphia. According to her autobiography, "I again stayed in Dr. Elder's family, and endeavored to increase my slender finances by dis-

Elizabeth Blackwell, M.D.

Bronze sculpture by A.E. Ted Aub. Courtesy Hobart and William Smith Colleges.

posing of some stories I had written, and by obtaining music pupils."
(Judging by the lengthy letters she wrote, writing was no great effort
for her. Later in life, she became a prolific writer.)

Blackwell decided to spend the summer at the huge Blockley
Almshouse of Philadelphia, where she was given a room in the women's
syphilitic department. Syphilis was then a serious disease, there being
no treatment until 1910. She noted that most of the women were unmarried, a large proportion seduced by the masters of the homes where
they worked as domestics. "All this is horrible! Women must really open
their eyes to it. I am convinced that they must regulate the matter. But
how?" A few months later, she mentioned in a letter that she would not
be blind, indifferent or stupid in relation to licentiousness, as were most
women. Years would pass before her mind "fully comprehended the
hideousness of modern fornication," but it is clear that her experience
at Blockley influenced her much later crusade against prostitution and
venereal disease.

Some newly arrived immigrants from Ireland were admitted to
Blockley that summer with so-called "ship fever." It was probably
typhus fever, but at the time the causative organism had not been iso-
lated. Blackwell chose to write her graduation thesis, due the second
term at Geneva, on the fever she saw at Blockley.

January 23, 1849, was graduation day for Blackwell. Of her days as
a medical student, she would write: "The behavior of the medical class
during the two years I was with them was admirable. It was that of true
Christian gentlemen."

Margaret Munro DeLancey, a Geneva resident, wrote to her sis-
ter-in-law about the graduation ceremony. Referring to Blackwell as
the "Lioness of the Day," she commented on the large number of curious women present. Miss DeLancey reported that Elizabeth was escorted
by her brother Henry, that on receiving her degree from the president,
she said, "I thank you, sir. It shall be the effort of my life, by God's bless-
ing, to shed honor on this diploma." Amid enthusiastic applause, Elizabeth Blackwell, M.D., bowed, blushed scarlet and left the stage to take
her seat among the graduates.

Kenyon Blackwell, a prosperous British cousin, was visiting in
Cincinnati. He, among others, encouraged her to obtain further training in Europe. Apparently some American physicians believed that
women doctors would be formidable competition and therefore tried
to prevent their entrance to training in clinics and hospitals. Elizabeth's
knowledge was largely theoretical — she had never even delivered a

baby — so she took the advice, assuming that the situation would be better on the other side of the Atlantic. She sailed from Boston on April 18, arriving in Liverpool 11 days later.

Before leaving, Blackwell applied for American citizenship. It was granted on April 13, 1849, when she became the second woman to become an American through naturalization. Despite this action, her writings gave the impression that she preferred England to the United States.

Blackwell visited her native country for a little longer than three weeks. She went sightseeing and also had the opportunity to visit St. Thomas Hospital. She then journeyed to Paris.

Her first concern was to become more facile at French. She was soon joined by her sister Anna, who was beginning to make a career for herself as a journalist. Elizabeth found that the classes she desired to attend were not open to her as a woman. After some deliberation, she applied to La Maternité as a student in midwifery and entered on June 30. This state-owned lying-in hospital was founded in 1615. In Blackwell's day, it was located in a former abbey. There were some 3,000 deliveries a year, most of the patients being unmarried women from the provinces. Some were poor women from Paris; some were prostitutes.

As early as 1820, Robert Collins of Dublin's Rotunda Hospital had recognized the contagious nature of puerperal fever. By 1843, Oliver Wendell Holmes, Sr., had published *Contagiousness of Puerperal Fever*, and four years later in Vienna, Hungarian Ignaz Semmelweiss found that the disease could be controlled if doctors routinely washed their hands with an antiseptic solution. However, some 30 years would pass before Louis Pasteur could convince the medical profession that the causative organism was a streptococcus. Thus, in 1849, La Maternité had frequent deaths from puerperal fever.

The students had many restrictions. Blackwell wrote to her mother, "I feel I shall gain a great deal, and hitherto it has really not proved so formidable an imprisonment as I supposed." She learned so much during the first three months that she arranged to stay three more before seeking the training that would make her a surgeon.

Her letters at this time paint an interesting picture of events at the institution. Here is a description of eight infants born the night before, arranged side by side.

> Each little shapeless red visage peeped from under a coarse
> peaked cap, on the front of which was a large label with the name

and sex; a black serge jacket with a white handkerchief pinned across, and a small blanket tightly folded round the back of the baby, completed the appearance of the little mummy.

During her fourth month at the institution, Blackwell syringed a baby's infected eye. Some of the contaminated water spurted into her own left eye, causing a serious infection that ultimately destroyed the vision in that eye. The accident forced Blackwell to leave La Maternité.

As part of her convalescence, she tried hydrotherapy — a fad cure at the time — in Grafenberg. Of course it did nothing for the blind eye, but the regimen prescribed seemed to improve her general health. When the eye became inflamed again, she returned to Paris. An eye specialist removed the diseased eye and later fitted a glass one.

Blackwell became reconciled to the fact that with impaired sight, she should abandon her plan to become a surgeon. Kenyon Blackwell had obtained permission for her to visit and study at St. Bartholomew's Hospital in London. The dean was the eminent James Paget, who later described two conditions, Paget's disease of the breast and Paget's disease of bone. Elizabeth attended his lectures on pathology. She spent three or four hours a day in the wards — chiefly medical — making diagnoses, watching the progress of cases and using the stethoscope.

She was also able to enjoy the company of a group of progressive and intellectual women who admired her achievement. This included Lady Byron, estranged wife and then widow of the poet, the feminist Barbara Leigh Smith (Bodichon), Barbara's cousin Florence Nightingale and George Eliot. Blackwell declared that she chiefly "owed the awakening to the fact that sanitation is the supreme goal of medicine, its foundation and its crown" to Florence Nightingale.

A letter written during this period to a sister notes Blackwell's concern with prostitution, which showed itself "so *publicly*" in London. "My great dream is of a grand moral reform society, a wide movement in this matter.... It would be a way to redeem the coming generation; education would be the keynote to change."

After about nine months, Blackwell decided it was time for her to practice in the United States. Although she had learned much abroad, she realized that many of the conventional treatments of the day were ineffective. This was an era in which leeches and purges were used as standard treatment, and "heresies" such as mesmerism came and went.

She sailed from Liverpool on July 26, 1851. A poor sailor, she did not care for ocean voyages. The departure date was later than she had anticipated, so she took advantage of the extra time to visit a cotton mill in Manchester, where she noted 800 looms at work in one room, mostly tended by women and very young girls. She wrote that the noise was tremendous, the dirt and heat oppressive.

According to Blackwell, "My first seven years of New York life were years of very difficult, though steady, uphill work." She had a good address, but patients came slowly, making her financial state precarious. She economized in many ways, but her means of support is often not clear; apparently relatives sometimes helped, occasionally wealthy friends.

In the spring of 1852, Blackwell lectured on *The Laws of Life with Special Reference to the Physical Education of Girls.* The lectures were popular with a group of Quaker friends who in time became her patients.

When her application to work in the women's department of a large city dispensary was refused, she decided to establish her own dispensary. By 1853, with the aid of friends, a small room was engaged in a slum area near Tompkins Square. The aim was to give needy women — many of them German immigrants — an opportunity to choose physicians of their own sex, even if the dispensary could remain open only three afternoons a week. There were male trustees and male consulting physicians, despite the fact that some members of the medical profession stood aloof from a female physician. This dispensary soon moved to Third Street.

In October 1854, Blackwell found Catherine "Kitty" Barry among 400 orphaned or destitute children at the immigrant depot at Randall's Island. In a letter to her sister Emily, Elizabeth referred to the 7-and-a-half-year-old Barry as "whom I mean to train up into a valuable domestic." However, for all practical purposes, she adopted the little Irish girl, but without changing her name, and saw that she obtained a good education. Barry remained fiercely loyal to Blackwell, and there seems to have been genuine affection between them. Barry never married, perhaps being expected to follow the course of Blackwell and her sisters. She became deaf, which made it difficult for her to meet new people.

That same year, 1854, Emily Blackwell had graduated from the medical school at Western Reserve University in Cleveland. She was fortunate in becoming an assistant to Dr. James Simpson, professor of midwifery at the University of Edinburgh. (He was especially noted for his use of chloroform in obstetrics.) After additional training abroad, Emily would join her sister in practice.

Meanwhile, Blackwell had met Marie Zakrzewska, an immigrant who would become her medical partner for a short time. Zakrzewska was born in Berlin in 1829. Her mother had been a midwife, and Zakrzewska graduated in 1851 from an outstanding Prussian midwifery school. A year later, she was appointed the chief midwife. After the death of the physician who was her mentor, she came to New York with aspirations of entering medical school. German doctors advised that she become a nurse, a course that Zakrzewska rejected. Visiting the Home for the Friendless to get advice, she was directed to Blackwell.

Since Zakrzewska's English was limited, Blackwell tutored her in the language. Zakrzewska in turn assisted at the dispensary. Admitted to Emily Blackwell's alma mater through Elizabeth's efforts, Zakrzewska obtained her doctorate in 1856. When she failed to find a landlord who would rent office space to a female physician, Blackwell supplied quarters in the 15th Street house that she had purchased. Some writers have suggested that both Blackwell and Zakrzewska had difficulty in renting suitable real estate because, as women doctors, they were considered abortionists.

Blackwell dreamed of creating a hospital to serve the indigent, to train efficient nurses and to provide adequate clinical training for female physicians who were barred from many facilities where good teaching was available. With the participation of her sister Emily and Zakrzewska, she had high hopes that her dream would materialize.

The New York Infirmary for Indigent Women and Children did open in May 1857, becoming the first hospital in the United States to be staffed by women. (There was a board of male consulting physicians.) Bed cases were accepted; the dispensary was open every morning; house calls were made. For the next two years, Zakrzewska worked without salary as resident physician and general manager of the hospital, supporting herself through her private practice. Zakrzewska described Blackwell as a "most womanly woman, delicate in size and figure, timid and reserved in manner, and modest in speech."

The original location of the hospital was 64 Bleeker Street. Those who could afford it were charged $4 per week, but most were unable to pay. Under such circumstances, there was a constant need to raise money. Some relief came in 1860, when the New York legislature granted the institution $1,000 per annum. That same year there was a move to Second Street on the corner of 8th. The services were gradually expanded. For example, by 1866, the infirmary had a "sanitary visitor" to advise families in their homes about cleanliness, infant care and so on. In 1876, the plant was moved again to Stuyvesant Square. Today it exists as New York Downtown Hospital, a teaching facility with 300 beds, serving some 60,000 people annually.

In 1858, Blackwell tried to raise funds for the Infirmary in England. She renewed old friendships and made new ones. She also became the first woman to be listed in the British Medical Register.

With the advent of the Civil War, Elizabeth and Emily called a meeting at the infirmary to discuss the training of women who volunteered to become nurses. A Women's Central Association of Relief was set up and Elizabeth was appointed to interview and select women for a short training period at one of three hospitals in New York City. Dorothea Dix, noted for her reform measures on behalf of the insane, was appointed superintendent of female nurses of the army. Elizabeth referred to her in a letter as being "without system, or any practical knowledge of the business." Elizabeth, nevertheless, sent Miss Dix names that represented "a good amount of excellent material out of the mass that presented itself." She also lectured to nurse trainees.

Elizabeth and Emily (Zakrzewska, too) were convinced that equality in medical education for men and women would become a fact if male physicians had some examples of well-trained female physicians rather than graduates of "quack" medical schools — those that stressed homeopathy, hydrotherapy, et cetera, and were likely to admit women. With this end in view and to provide more immediate opportunities to women, the Women's Medical College of the New York Infirmary was founded in 1868, due to much effort on Elizabeth's part. It continued until 1899. One of the first colleges in the United States to mandate first a three-year and then a four-year program, it had high standards. By 1899, when the school closed, there were 422 graduates. The students enrolled were transferred to Cornell University Medical College, which was accepting women like many other recognized institutions.

Since hygiene was the keynote of Elizabeth's concept of medicine, she made herself the lecturer in that field. Emily became the professor of obstetrics and diseases of women. Elizabeth's tenure was brief; in July 1869, she sailed for England, where she remained most of her life. Emily shouldered responsibility for both the school and infirmary. From Kitty Barry's recollections, there is reason to suppose that there was friction between the sisters. Elizabeth's official explanation was, "In 1869 the early pioneer work in America was ended." She intended to assist the same cause in England and Scotland.

Elizabeth involved herself for many years in social reform by lecturing and writing. In 1876 she lectured at the newly established London School of Medicine for Women, but in 1877 resigned her lectureship. Her social life was pleasant — it involved acquaintances such as Herbert Spencer, Gabriel Rosetti and Charles Kingsley. She found time to travel on the continent. She seems to have lived on investments made in the United States.

Blackwell's writings include *The Religion of Health* (1871), *Counsel to Parents in the Moral Education of Their Children* (1878), *The Human Element in Sex* (1884); the autobiographical *Pioneer Work in Opening the Medical Profession to Women* (1895) and *Essays in Medical Sociology* (1902). *Counsel to Parents* was the best known, being published in the United States as well as Britain. These works covered hygiene, medical education and religion, with her primary focus on sexual ethics. An advocate of the repeal of the British Communicable Disease Acts (which provided for police regulation of prostitution), she emphasized a single standard in sexual matters.

In 1883, Blackwell purchased a home — Rock House — in Hastings on the English Channel. Here she and Barry spent many happy years. Blackwell even involved herself in local politics.

Despite her tendency to become seasick she returned to the United States in 1906 for a visit with her family. She died of a stroke in Hastings in 1910 at the age of 89.

Elizabeth Blackwell deserves great credit for her perseverance in obtaining a medical degree from a recognized institution. Her family connections undoubtedly helped her to secure necessary letters of introduction to influential persons; the Blackwell family's proclivity to involve themselves in righteous causes must have inspired her. But she alone was responsible for the required steadfastness. She realized the importance of good clinical training if women physicians were to help women patients, and she worked to make that training possible in the United States.

Blackwell warned against blind acceptance of "authority" in medicine. She realized that the medicine of her day was "an uncertain science." Her emphasis on hygiene and preventive medicine was progressive for her day. However, her writings showed that she had little regard for the germ theory of disease, which is vital to an understanding of preventive medicine. She was opposed to smallpox vaccination; an antivivisectionist, she deplored the use of the Pasteur treatment for rabies because it caused suffering to dogs. (Less than 12 years after her death, purified insulin was administered to a severe diabetic for the first time without side-effects. Many animals were sacrificed in the process of producing this life-saving product, but a Nobel Prize was awarded to those who made insulin available.)

Author Mary Roth Walsh has observed that nineteenth-century women, out of a sense of indelicacy, either avoided medical attention entirely or concealed difficulties from their doctors. Queen Victoria wrote to her daughter Vicky about "humiliations to the delicate feelings of a poor woman, above all a young one — especially with those nasty doctors." To cite another example, Samuel Gregory, founder of the Boston Female Medical College, described male midwifery as an indecency, declaring, "So the physician, by constant familiarity, comes to consider female delicacy and reserve as not worth preserving." Considering such attitudes, Blackwell's crusade to recruit female physicians is laudable.

Her former coworker, Marie Zakrzewska, wrote:

> Nobody has fathomed the depth of Dr. Elizabeth Blackwell's soul as I have had the opportunity to do ... she seemed to me a prophet of no ordinary insight and foresight.... To me she was, and is, not preeminently the physician but the philanthropic philosopher, the standard bearer of a higher womanhood.

Lilly Martin Spencer

Lilly Martin Spencer was a successful painter. A pragmatist, she painted what the public wanted; she also satisfied her artistic ambitions by producing an allegory entitled "Truth Unveiling Falsehood." Aside from her professional life, Mrs. Spencer had seven children who depended largely on her for support. In 1842 she said, "...our own feet are yet the best to stand on, bad as they may be, for if we do on others, we will be likely to be tripped."

She was born on November 26, 1822, in Exeter, England, to Giles Martin and Angelique Perrine (le Petit) Martin, the eldest of four. Originally from Brittany, the parents had come to Exeter, where the father taught French. The family next emigrated to New York City, remaining there for two years. They then settled permanently near Marietta, Ohio. Giles Martin secured a position as a teacher of French in the institution that would become Marietta College.

Lilly, christened Angelique Marie, was raised and taught at home in an atmosphere of culture and liberal ideas. Her well-educated parents were followers of Charles Fourier, the French social philosopher who evolved a kind of utopian socialism; they favored abolition and woman suffrage.

The Martin home was located outside Marietta on 150 acres of land. *The Marietta Intelligence* of 1839 reported that young Lilly used the plaster walls of the home to execute charcoal drawings. Her murals continued to attract attention for some time. Apparently they were covered at a later date.

It is clear that the Martin parents encouraged their daughter's talent. In New York City she had attended art classes at the old Academy of Design. In Ohio she came into contact with two trained artists. One was Sala Bosworth, who painted portraits and local landscapes. The other was Charles Sullivan, a student of Thomas Scully and a landscape painter. It appears that these men introduced Lilly to oil painting; the first exhibition of her oil paintings was held in the Sullivan home.

Related to Lilly's training as an artist was a spirit of self-sufficiency, partly fostered by the Martins and exhibited at an early age in the young painter.

She was 18 when she first showed a collection of her works in a church basement near her home. The daytime admission was 25 cents and in the evening, "with music in attendance," the fee was 37½ cents. The charge was to defray Martin's expenses in Cincinnati, where she was about to go for additional education. The exhibit reflected her broad interests, among them portraits of local persons, depictions of family events and scenes from literature.

With low attendance, the admission fees brought in little money. However, the exhibit caught the attention of Edward Mansfield, editor of the *Cincinnati Chronicle*, who was visiting Marietta. He viewed the murals and wrote favorably in the *Marietta Intelligence* of Martin's efforts. Through him she was put in contact with Nicholas Longworth, a Cincinnati patron of the arts and benefactor. He offered to finance her instruction by teachers on the East Coast. Later Longworth proposed sending Martin to Europe to study — copying old masters instead of concentrating on original work.

Martin declined both offers, for speculative reasons. She was possibly influenced by the spirit of nativism that was present in the era. This attitude is exemplified by "Rules for Picture-Buying," which first appeared in the New York *Tribune* and was reprinted in 1851 in *The Crayon*. Buyers were urged always to prefer a modern to an old picture; they were reminded that there were excellent artists in their own country and that these people should be supported in preference to foreign artists.

It should be noted that Martin's self-image may have been involved in her thinking. In 1847, she wrote her parents that she intended to become a Michael Angelo (sic), if she possibly could. Five years earlier, she had written her mother that she wanted her work to tend to moral improvement. Ann Bird Schumer, in her master's thesis, reported that Martin's reaction to one of Benjamin West's paintings was, "It is most beautiful, but I think that I could do as well..." Benjamin West was a noted historical painter of the time.

In November 1841, Martin moved to Cincinnati to further her education and to earn money. Her father stayed with her for a short time before returning to Marietta. She was an experienced portrait painter, having produced more than 50 portraits. Her exhibit, when moved from Marietta to Cincinnati, prompted the editor of the *Cincinnati Daily Gazette* to refer to Martin's "extraordinary talent." No doubt she expected good financial returns from commissions. But success came slowly. In the late spring of 1842, Giles Martin came back to Cincinnati to give private French lessons. One person whom he instructed was an artist named John Insco Williams. In exchange for French lessons, Williams taught Lilly. Little is known about the arrangement. It is known that the Martins continued to encourage and support their daughter to a degree that was unusual for the day.

While in Cincinnati, Martin appears to have known James H. Beard, an artist of some note. How much influence he had on her is not clear. Three years passed before she experienced limited success in the form of commissions and exhibitions.

In 1844, Lilly married Benjamin Rush Spencer, who had emigrated to Virginia from England. There is some evidence that he belonged to the British nobility. Moving to Cincinnati following a business failure, he was once an importer of cloth. He did not seem to prosper in any business, but made a good househusband. Seven Spencer children reached maturity, although Lilly had 13 pregnancies between 1845 and 1866. According to Diane J. Dykema's master's thesis, Benjamin, in addition to supervising the children, made frames for his wife's pictures, delivered her finished works and tried to negotiate as her agent. Little is known about this man, but the marriage seems to have been a happy one. In view of the high value that Lilly set on self-sufficiency, the arrangement she had with Ben, as she called him, seemed to suit her needs.

From 1846 on, Spencer was recognized as one of Cincinnati's best artists. That year saw the founding of the Western Art Union. Spencer joined and in 1847 had eight paintings at the opening exhibit. Members of art unions paid a fee, for which they received a periodical devoted to art, a free reproduction of a famous painting and the opportunity to participate in a lottery of original art works.

Seeking better recompense and recognition, Spencer considered making her home in Columbus, Ohio, but that did not materialize. Instead the family moved to New York City in 1848. (She had already exhibited "The Water Spirit" at the National Academy of Design in that city.) After the move, she exhibited and sold her works through the American Art Union and its successor, the Cosmopolitan Art Association. A letter written in 1850 stated that the Art Union was the chief point — indeed almost the only one — for the sale of her pictures.

Lilly Martin Spencer

"Self Portrait." Courtesy Ohio Historical Society.

In 1849, the Western Art Union arranged to pay Alfred Jones of New York City $1,200 to make an engraving of "One of Life's Happy Hours" by Spencer. She had, at an earlier date, sold the painting to Charles Stetson, president of the Union. He loaned it to make the engraving, and Spencer received nothing. Since the engraving was used as the Union's free gift, it brought her publicity, if not money. This graphic reproduction was one of many colored lithographs and etchings to come, produced from Spencer's works. Between 1820 and 1880, Americans treasured lithographs, which were made by printing from a plain surface on which the image to be printed is ink-receptive and the blank area ink-repellent.

The three-volume *Women of the American Revolution* by Elizabeth F. Ellet came out in 1850, with portions of its text and artwork reproduced in *Godey's Lady's Book*. According to authorities, the illustrations were made by Spencer. (The fourth edition has illustrations but no attribution, a situation that was apparently not uncommon in the nineteenth century.)

At the 1852 exhibition of the American Art-Union, Spencer's paintings sold for more than those of John James Audubon, whose paintings of birds were very popular. It was fortunate that she had gained such acclaim, because by that time, lottery-based litigation against the art unions was bringing about their demise.

Spencer's success was largely dependent on her depictions of domestic scenes, especially those that represented childhood. By mid–nineteenth century, the public had accepted the child as a unique and innocent individual, not a small adult in whom evil should be suppressed. Spencer's appealing children were in accord with this concept. Her family provided ideas and models — for example, her 1857 "Listening to Father's Watch" showed Benjamin and their son William.

"Shake Hands" was executed in 1854. Three years later, the *Cosmopolitan Art Journal* noted:

> "Shake Hands" is already familiar from the Paris lithograph made of it, and from the exhibiting of it in Cincinnati, New York, etc. It is one of the few pictures whose popularity increases with every exhibition.... Perhaps no picture painted in this country is better fitted for popular appreciation.

As emphasized by Schumer, Spencer was often regarded as a "nursery" painter, mainly because so many of the children she painted were reproduced in the form of engravings and hand-tinted lithographs. However, she received many private commissions to paint, for instance, the portrait of Mayor Morris of New York City. (There is now documented evidence that she painted many notables, including Generals Grant and Sherman, Washington Irving, Martin Van Buren and Ella Wheeler Wilcox.) During her residence in New York, she probably painted "Algeria," which she considered a masterpiece. Based on a poem by Byron, it was sold to Elias Howe, the inventor of the sewing machine. As with many of Spencer's paintings, it has disappeared. The fact that she often neglected to sign or date her works makes them hard to trace. There is reason to believe that many were sold in England by one of the Spencer daughters.

The Spencers made another move in 1858 — this time to Newark, New Jersey. The family's first residence there belonged to Marcus L. Ward, a relative to Nicholas Longworth. In lieu of rent, Spencer was to paint two designated portraits and "one handsome fancy piece." She would remain in Newark for some 20 years. Spencer continued to paint; in 1860, an art journal commented that her pictures commanded high prices and were worth the money.

During the Newark period, Spencer was engaged in her most ambitious project — the allegorical "Truth Unveiling Falsehood." She worked on it in a rented studio in Manhattan for three years. (Persons such as William Cullen Bryant and Henry Ward Beecher gathered at this studio.) Completed in 1869, the 8-foot high painting was rented by a New York firm. It was insured by Lloyd's of London for $20,000, the amount twice offered to Lilly for it. The rental fee was $150 a week. It was exhibited in the Women's Pavilion at the Centennial Exhibition in Philadelphia and then at the subsequent Permanent International Exhibition until 1890. The whereabouts of "Truth Unveiling Falsehood" is not known today. Attempting to trace it, Schumer found only that it had been in storage from 1902 until 1951. A photograph of the work is extant. Here is part of Spencer's own explanation of her allegory:

> Truth is the centre figure. Falsehood on the left with Ignorance at its feet. On the right is Confidence resting against Truth, with Innocence in her lap. The Picture is intended to represent and contrast the beauty and power of Truth (under whose protection all that is good prospers), with the opposite results under the deceiving cover of Falsehood, where the monster Selfishness (originator of all man's evil passions) is enabled to destroy human trust and human Innocence, typified by a helpless babe entrusted to it by Ignorance, in which, and the consequent misery and degradation, it keeps mankind through its false attributes.

In 1880, the family moved to upstate New York. Spencer's popularity had declined and she was painting fewer works. The last exhibition

Lilly Martin Spencer

"Shake Hands." Courtesy Ohio Historical Society.

for which there is a record of her contribution was the Centennial of 1876. Four years later, Benjamin Spencer died.

Little is known about Spencer during the period 1880–1900. She did make a portrait of the famous agnostic, Robert C. Ingersoll, with two of his grandchildren. She appears to have been friendly with him, and some believe that she embraced his views. (This despite the fact that her father had once studied for the priesthood and her mother was educated in a convent.) Other subjects included Elizabeth Cady Stanton and Caroline Lavinia Scott Harrison, while she was First Lady.

Returning to New York City in 1900, Spencer reentered the art world. She died while working in her studio in 1902, at the age of 79. She was buried at Highland, New York, beside her husband.

Lilly Martin Spencer appears to have been considerably ahead of her time. Her non–American background may have contributed to her emancipated ideas; as a married woman with a large family, she seriously pursued a career. Dykema, writing in 1993, contended that Spencer could succeed as a professional artist as long as she proved she was a mother first or "womanly" artist who painted in an appropriate female genre. Whatever the reason, with very little training and, at the same time, great self-confidence, she was successful in that career — both financially and professionally. Her letters show that often the family had a meager existence; nevertheless, she managed to support them for years, standing on her own feet, as she expressed it. Many of her serious works received favorable critical acclaim. And her images of children appealed to thousands; in a way, they achieved her early goal of making painting a force to promote moral improvement.

An exhibition in 1973 at the Smithsonian Institution featured some of Spencer's paintings. Assistant curator Robin Bolton-Smith wrote about Lilly:

> ...her preoccupation with what she knew most intimately provided her with the basics of an art which, at its best, transcends the sentiment of her time. Aside from the pleasurable glimpse into the everyday life of a century ago, the paintings still provoke a sharpened appreciation of those humble facts that we might otherwise pass by.

Maria Kraus-Boelté

Maria Kraus-Boelté's life was intertwined with Froebel's method of kindergarten teaching—"a school for the psychological training of little children by means of play and occupations." To understand her contribution, some brief background history must be presented.

Friedrich Froebel was born in Oberweissbach, Thuringia, in 1782. His father was a Lutheran pastor and his mother died before he was a year old. His childhood was unhappy and his youth unsettled. At 23, however, he found his life's work in education. By 1837, at Blankenburg, Germany, he opened a school for children aged 3–7. Three years later, he named it a kindergarten.

Unfortunately for his contemporaries and for posterity, the style of Froebel's publications make for difficult reading. Modern educators have noted the essentials of Froebel's theory of education. For ages 4 through 6 or 7, he advocated systematic activity; playing with toys; playing games and singing songs; and gardening and caring for animals. He respected a child's individuality; he realized the importance of initiative; and he insisted on social relationships.

His philosophy of childhood education differed from that of most of his contemporaries, who looked on preschools as simple copies of regular schools, and who believed that children can be governed only by fear. In stark contrast to the grim atmosphere of the schools of his day, in his school a group of children could actually be happy while learning. It should be realized that Froebel's ideas on education did not pertain exclusively to the kindergarten years; his philosophy covered a long period of learning. Ironically, Froebel did not in the beginning consider the desirability of female teachers for his kindergarten.

Froebel's concepts were not entirely original; for example, as early as 1658, the Moravian educator John Amos Comenius had published a teaching device that was the first picture book for children. In addition,

Froebel's ideas were based on the teachings of Johann Heinrich Pestalozzi (1796–1827) and Jean Jacques Rousseau (1712–1778).

There had been other preschools, but they were not started with the premise that young children require unique education. To exemplify, in 1767, Johann Friedrich Oberlin, a native of Strasbourg, founded a type of infant school that years later became part of France's free educational system. Also in 1816, Robert Owen established a school in Scotland for children 18 months to 10 years old. Oberlin's school was for the offspring of parents who worked in the fields, while Owen's was for children of workers in cotton mills. In each case, social philanthropy was the motivating force and the school's primary function was the provision of babysitting.

A British report from 1853-54 regarding education noted that:

> So long as [infant schools] were regarded merely as places where children, assumed to be too young to benefit by instruction, were amused and kept safe from harm — as institutions which might claim, perhaps, the negative merit of preventing mischief, but certainly had no pretensions to be regarded as conferring positive benefit — it was natural that they should excite only secondary interest.

The Prussian government, convinced that Froebel's emphasis on self-activity and initiative was fostering revolutionary ideas, placed a ban on his school from 1851 to 1860. Chiefly through the efforts of the Baroness von Marenholtz-Bülow, his ideas spread posthumously to many countries, including the United States.

Maria Kraus-Boelté was born on November 8, 1836, at Hagenow in the grand duchy of Mecklenburg-Schwerin, Germany, to Ernst Boelté and Louise (Ehlers) Boelté. Her father was a lawyer and her mother came from a professional family. "Our parents were our best friends," Maria wrote. "We had more liberty than other children, and our family, though aristocratic, was often called 'the small Republic.'" They led a privileged existence, and unlike Froebel, Boelté enjoyed her childhood. According to her, "Although kindergartens were not yet in existence, the occupations which Froebel systematized in the existence, the occupations which Froebel systematized in the new education, were in requisition in the family nurture of our household." Among other memories, she recalled building with blocks, using beads for counting, dressing her 21 dolls with clothes she made herself, tending her own garden and using for gymnastics such apparatus as a climbing pole. At the same time, the Boelté children were taught "not to measure ourselves with others according to rank, pretty clothes, good home, etc., but rather according to our own worth."

Maria received a broad and thorough education, mostly from tutors. In addition, the Boelté home was a literary and musical center where prominent intellectuals gathered. A visit from a paternal aunt, Amély Boelté, had a profound effect on her niece's life. The former was a writer who, according to Maria, "regarded the woman's question as her special mission." Not impressed with the latter's carefree existence, Amely arranged for Maria to go to Hamburg to study the kindergarten method under Luise Levin Froebel, Friedrich's widow. During her two years in Hamburg, Boelté also met several persons who impressed her with their dedication to doing good works.

In 1849, Bertha Rongé, a pupil of Froebel, had been invited to Manchester, England, to organize a kindergarten there. After her stay in Hamburg, Boelté worked under the direction of this woman, first in Manchester and a short time later in London. This forced her to learn English. In London she taught in a kindergarten and also held more advanced classes, both without recompense, because the children were poor. During this time she made the acquaintance of Charles Dickens and Giuseppe Mazzini, the Italian patriot and revolutionist.

With Mrs. Rongé's return to Germany, Boelté found a teaching position with a prominent family in Kent. "I had the fullest swing to carry out my kindergarten ideas with ever so many big and little children," she wrote. (Mothers and children of the neighborhood were included in her classes.) The work of her charges was displayed at the London International Exhibition in 1862.

Boelté realized the importance of having teachers well trained in kindergarten methods. (In her day, such individuals were called kindergartners.) Dismayed by the public's poor understanding of true kindergarten methods, she devoted much of her energy for the next five years to the promotion of the kindergarten system as established by Froebel. This was done, to quote her, "without price."

In the autumn of 1867, Boelté returned to Hamburg, where for several months she was the guest of Johanna Goldschmidt, president of the Froebel Union and mother-in-law of singer Jennie Lind. Boelté visited kindergartens and taught at the Union.

Her next venture was to open a private kindergarten in Lübeck, the home of a married sister. Despite open opposition to kindergarten education, she started a class with seven children in October; by June she had 55. When Mrs. Froebel visited, she exclaimed, "Oh, that Froebel had known you — could have seen your work; you are, in truth, his spiritual daughter." Such praise encouraged Boelté and, for years to come, strengthened her resolve. She also trained teachers.

In November 1868, she was a delegate to the Women's Convention in Berlin. It was an opportunity to meet again with her aunt Amély, whom she had not seen for many years.

Gradually the Lübeck kindergarten won the approval of its former opponents. During the Franco-Prussian War (1870–71), the children raised money with a display and sale of their work. The proceeds, amounting to $100 benefitted both German and French wounded. Boelté closed the Lübeck school in 1871.

Froebel's ideas were first put into effect in the United States in 1855, when Margaretta Schurz, one of his pupils, established in Watertown, Wisconsin, the first German-speaking kindergarten in the country. Mrs. Schurz was the sister of Mrs. Rongé and the wife of Carl Schurz, the German-American political leader and reformer. As had happened in some other families, one of her motivations was the desire for her children to benefit from kindergarten training.

Five years later, Elizabeth Peabody started the nation's first English-speaking kindergarten in Boston, representing the Concord school of philosophy (transcendentalism). When she found that she was not following Froebel's concepts, she went to Germany to learn from true Froebel disciples. (One of Elizabeth Peabody's sisters was married to educator Horace Mann and another to Nathaniel Hawthorne.)

In 1870, Boelté began a correspondence with John Kraus, a German-born educator who had emigrated to the United States in 1851. He established schools and propagated Froebel methods. In 1867, Henry Bernard, America's first commissioner of the Bureau of Education, invited him to work with that department. During his tenure there, Kraus wrote an extensive report about the progress of the Froebel kindergarten in the United States. The correspondence stimulated Boelté's interest in spreading Froebel's gospel to the United States.

After Lübeck, Boelté returned to England for a brief stay. At the urging of Elizabeth Peabody, she emigrated in September 1872, to New York City to take a position in a private school conducted by Henrietta Haines. She immediately organized a kindergarten and mothers' class. The aim of this mothers' class was to make Froebel's ideas better understood.

In the same year, Susan Blow, who was somewhat familiar with German kindergarten methods, was considering the establishment of a kindergarten in St. Louis. Dr. William Harris, the superintendent of schools, supported her in this experiment, with the approval of the school board. It was agreed that Miss Blow should first have the necessary training. For this she went to New York to study under Boelté. Then in the fall of 1873, the nation's first public kindergarten opened in the Des Pres School in Carondelet, a suburb of St. Louis, where Susan Blow resided.

In 1873, when she was 37, Boelté married Professor John Kraus, the man who had corresponded with her about his report on Froebel. He was some 20 years her senior. Maria took as her last name Kraus-Boelté. Resigning from the Bureau of Education, Kraus worked with his wife to found the New York Seminary for Kindergartners. It had a model kindergarten. Later, lower primary grades and training classes for children's nurses were added. Kraus-Boelté was considered a strict disciplinarian of adult students, with formal manners, but also an inspiring and gifted teacher.

At a meeting of the National Education Association in Boston in 1872, she gave a complete explanation of the Froebel theory and method. She continued to keep the image of the kindergarten before the NEA. At the Centennial Convention in Baltimore in 1876, she lectured and exhibited kindergarten children's work. From 1899 to 1900, she served as president of the NEA's Kindergarten Department. It is noteworthy that at the organization's convention held in Toronto in 1891, the state superintendent of schools from New York proposed a resolution that was unanimously carried: that kindergarten be recommended as a part of all school systems.

In 1877, the Krauses published an influential work, *The Kindergarten Guide*. This two-volume book with numerous illustrations explained philosophy, aims and methods. The authors stressed that it was Froebel's contention that his system of educational development should be continued beyond the kindergarten age of the child.

In 1890, model kindergarten classes at the Seminary were dropped to give more time for training future kindergarten teachers. After Professor Kraus died in 1896, Kraus-Boelté continued this work alone until she retired in 1913. She wrote papers and lectured to make her cause known.

She was responsible for obtaining college credit for kindergarten teaching. In the summer session of 1903, New York University's School

Maria Kraus-Boelté

Copied from Pioneers of the Kindergarten in America.

20   NEW YORK UNIVERSITY

S25. Kindergarten Methods   10.30–12.30
MRS. MARIA KRAUS-BOELTÉ.

In order to meet the needs of many students who are unable to be present during the entire six weeks of the Summer School, Kindergarten methods will be presented in two courses, each meeting two hours a day for three weeks. The *First Course*, commencing July 6 and ending July 27, will include subjests concerning the field of the usual kindergarten training. The Kindergarten Gifts, Occupations, Games, Songs, Marches, Stories, Garden-work, Sand-table, etc., will be viewed somewhat in detail, with practical illustrations. In the *Second Course*, commencing July 28 and continuing until the end of Summer School, August 16, will give a more general treatment of Kindergarten subjects, including Froebel's Pedagogics ; Mother-Play ; some History of Education lectures ; the social, ethical and religious training of children ; self-activity ; the psychological and physiological basis of Froebel's education ; the " Education of Man," etc.

Students of the first course will find it advantageous to provide themselves with a " set " of kindergarten materials, both Gifts and Occupations.

Froebel's "Mother-Play book " and " Education of Man" are recommended to students of the second course.

Both courses will include practical exercises of rhythm, songs and games. The University Gymnasium will be open for students of the Kindergarten courses daily until 1 P.M.

The work of each course is complete in itself, so that either may be taken alone, but University credit is given only in case both courses are completed. Students taking one course will be charged the fee for a one hour course ($15.00). Students taking both courses will be charged the usual tuition fee ($25.00), which fee admits to all courses the student may elect, subject to the approval of the Faculty.

Maria Kraus-Boelté

Course description of "Kindergarten Methods" taught by Maria Kraus-Boelté in 1904. Courtesy Office of University Archives, New York University.

of Education offered a course in kindergarten education with Kraus-Boelté as instructor. This course was repeated in 1904 and 1907.

    Kraus-Boelté died of cancer in 1918, just before her 82nd birthday. She was survived by an adopted daughter.

    For many years, Kraus-Boelté worked assiduously to present true Froebel philosophy. This brought her recognition as an authority on the subject. Pure Froebelian methods would be promoted by Susan Blow and her followers; proponents of a more flexible system would be led by Patty Hill Smith (1868–1946). In 1912, Dr. Maria Montessori's theory took root in the United States: it aimed at reversing the traditional system of an active teacher instructing a passive class. Thus the kindergarten system continued to grow, change — and flourish.

More than 1,200 young women and 2,000 children in this country came under the influence of Maria Kraus-Boelté, the disciple of a German educator. She lived to see free kindergartens become part of most educational systems in her adopted country.

Anna Howard Shaw

Anna Howard Shaw was an ordained minister who had her own interpretation of St. Paul's injunction (I Timothy 2:12) to "suffer not a woman to teach, nor to usurp authority over the man, but to be in silence." Women preachers, although rare in the mid–nineteenth century were not unknown among some denominations in the United States. By 1851, the United Brethren had even ordained a woman. Nevertheless, it was still unusual for a woman to enter the clergy.

Anna Howard Shaw was born in Newcastle upon Tyne in England on February 14, 1847. Her mother, Nicolas (Stott) Shaw, and father, Thomas Shaw, were of Scottish descent. Her maternal grandmother was one of the first Unitarians in England, gaining family distinction because she refused to pay tithes to the established Church of England, and as a result, saw her possessions sold to pay the obligation.

At the time of Anna's birth (she was known as Annie for many years), her family was trying to pay off debts. Although Thomas Shaw's trade involved the staining and embossing of wall paper, he had gone into the flour and grain business, in which he had failed because of the repeal of the protective Corn Laws. His wife took in sewing, at which she was particularly skilled, and the hope was that when their debts were paid, the family — mother, father and six children — would emigrate to the United States.

Thomas Shaw left first, and then in 1851, the others followed in a sailing ship bound for New York. Misinformed that the ship had sunk and there were no survivors, Shaw was not there to meet his family. He soon learned the welcome news that his wife and children were in New York, and hastened there.

He had found work in New Bedford, Massachusetts, but the following year moved the family to Lawrence. The Shaws remained in this progressive Massachusetts town until 1859, and Anna recalled becoming interested in the abolition movement during that time. They were Unitarians, and through their church they knew Robert Shaw, who would become colonel of 54th Massachusetts Regiment, the first body of Negro troops raised in a free state. She remembered seeing an escaped slave hidden in the coal bin of the family residence. Like thousands of her day, she read *Uncle Tom's Cabin*. Also in her Lawrence experience was her childhood acquaintance with a woman who was a prostitute. Anna liked to visit this woman, who loved her. The Shaws were tolerant enough to permit such visits, and Anna credited her later understanding of and sympathy for "fallen women" to this Lawrence resident.

Life changed for Anna when she was 12. Her father received a grant of 360 acres in the wilderness of Michigan. With the aid of James, his 20-year-old son, he cleared a small space and made a cabin. Then he returned to Lawrence, arranging that his wife, James, one young son, two daughters and Anna remain at the cabin to hold the Michigan claim. He planned to continue to work in Massachusetts — as did the two sons — and send whatever he could to support the family in the wilderness.

Near what is currently Big Rapids, the site of the cabin was 150 miles from Grand Rapids, where the railway terminated. Of course conditions were very primitive. The cabin was unchinked; there was a dirt floor; the furniture was yet to be made; water had to be hauled from a creek — and so on. Mrs. Shaw seems to have been a chronic invalid when she arrived. Now the conditions in her new home did not contribute to her mental health, for she was a practical individual who realized how self-sufficient her children would have to be to survive. Her superior ability in sewing did mean that they had good clothing.

During the first winter, the family subsisted largely on corn meal bought from a mill 20 miles distant. They owned a cow, which provided milk. (Later, when it died, they went without milk for months.) The source of water was melted snow. To add to their discomfort, they constantly feared the wild animals they heard in the forest and they dreaded attack by drunken Ottawa Indians.

When spring came, the resourceful Anna, with help from a young neighbor, constructed a well. In summer, wild berries were abundant and fish could be caught with improvised equipment such as wires from hoop skirts. There were no horses for ploughing, and tree stumps abounded, but after planting seeds under sod chopped up by ax, the Shaws eventually had good corn and potatoes.

When Thomas Shaw joined his family, James had been gone for

some months, forced by illness to go east. The elder Shaw was a visionary and was devoted to his family, but he had no practical knowledge of farming and thus was of little help to their frontier existence. Anna gave an example of this: He spent time during planting season in predicting the production of a certain number of kernels of corn rather than actually planting the corn.

With the nearest school some ten miles away, Anna learned at home from books brought from Lawrence and from reading material sent by her father. When she was 13, a school three miles from home opened. She attended for a short time, but soon decided that the six-mile-a-day walk was not worth the effort, since she knew more than the teacher.

By the time she was 14, Shaw knew she wanted to preach — according to her, "to talk to people, to tell them things." She had practiced in the woods, addressing the unresponsive trees. No doubt her taste of pioneer life had left her with new confidence and independence that later would serve her well.

At 15, a self-taught Shaw was teaching a school for 14 pupils of various ages. She received $2 per week and was entitled to "boarding round" in pupils' homes because the school's location was four miles from the Shaw cabin. As was usual at the time, the teacher was responsible for seeing that the schoolhouse's wood stove had fuel; books were in short supply; and long distances had to be walked from boarding home to school. Shaw recalled that the $26 she earned for the 13-week session was held up until the dog tax was collected in the spring.

Her wages improved as time passed, but so did her obligations. With the advent of the Civil War, her brothers and father enlisted, leaving her as the principal support of the family. "It was," she recalled, "an incessant struggle to keep our land, to pay our taxes and to live.... There were no men left to grind our corn, to get in our crops, or to care for our livestock."

When the war ended and the men returned, Shaw had opportunity to pursue her own interests. Apparently marriage did not enter the picture; she was going to college, and she began to save for it. The year 1870 saw her living in Big Rapids with her sister Mary, whose husband offered their home. Encouraged by a universalist female minister named Marianna Thompson, Shaw entered Big Rapids High School to prepare for college and ultimately preaching. Here, at the age of 23, she learned election and enrolled in speaking and debating classes.

It was especially fortunate for her that the presiding elder of the district wanted to have a woman ordained for the Methodist ministry, and he promoted her as that candidate. Her first step was to preach at a quarterly meeting in Ashton, Michigan. This she did successfully enough to be invited by the elder to preach at 36 different locations in his circuit. At the district's annual Methodist Conference she was voted a license to preach.

Shaw's determination to follow a career considered unsuitable for a woman caused a rift with her family, who offered to pay her college expenses if she would forgo the pulpit. But she was not to be deterred from her chosen course. On the other hand, she received encouragement from the suffragist and reformer, Mary Livermore, who came to lecture in Big Rapids.

The fall of 1873 saw Shaw at Albion (Mi.) College. For the first year, she was fortunate in finding board at the home of the president and his wife for $4 per week. Tuition was provided for a licensed preacher, and she occasionally made $5 for a lecture on temperance. But the financial uncertainty was stressful to her.

Shaw was soon selected as orator at a reunion of literary societies. Her family members were sufficiently impressed to provide a beautiful gown for the occasion.

She spent the following summer at St. Johnsbury, Vermont, at the home of James. The latter arranged for his sister to preach at the local church, and this led to similar invitations to nearby parishes.

The second year at Albion went well, with enough preaching to cover her expenses.

In the summer of 1874, Shaw agreed to substitute for a minister in a lumber camp. She arrived at Seberwaing by stagecoach late on a Saturday. She found a man who would drive her through the woods to her destination. After dark and when they were well into the forest, she realized that the driver had anything but honorable intentions toward her. She drew a revolver from her handbag, cocked it, then aimed it at his back, and ordered him to drive on. She threatened to shoot if he stopped or spoke. Realizing that she meant what she said, he delivered her safely at dawn to the log hotel where she was to stay.

In February 1876, Shaw entered the School of Theology at Boston University. Nearing 30, she felt pressed to accomplish her goal as soon as possible. Male licensed preachers in the entering class were given free dormitory accommodation while board at a club cost $1.25 per week. Shaw was given $2 per week to arrange her own rent and board. Competition for employment as a substitute preacher was great among her classmates, and the result was that she often went hungry for periods of time. An anonymous donor eventually came forward, providing money for adequate meals.

On Sundays she attended the churches of Phillips Brooks and James Freeman Clarke. The former, author of "O Little Town of Bethlehem," was associated with Boston's Trinity Episcopal Church, and the latter with Boston's Unitarian Church of the Disciples.

Shaw also worked with "fallen women." According to her autobiography, "I soon learned that the effective work in that field is the work which is done for women before, not after they have fallen."

As the only woman in a class of 43, she felt that she was not wanted. However, she remained, obtaining a Doctor of Divinity degree in 1878.

During the summer of 1876, Shaw filled in at some pulpits on Cape Cod. In East Dennis she formed a friendship with a wealthy widow named Persis Addey. A year later, Mrs. Addey died of a brain tumor. The two women had planned a European tour, and Mrs. Addey's will provided money for Shaw to proceed as they had intended. Thus following graduation, Shaw joined a European tour that lasted for three months. This was the first of many times she would visit Europe.

Her first pastorate was in East Dennis, where she spent seven years. She inherited a congregation divided over a long-standing issue. Refusing to listen to verbal complaints, she suggested that each side present its case in writing. Both declined to do this, but each tried to make its point during public prayer — referring to a parishioner by name and then labeling him as a liar or a slanderer, and adding details that Shaw had requested in writing. No doubt she was amused by this, for she was blessed with a good sense of humor. However, after the third prayer meeting, she put a stop to the activity that was making her church the laughing stock of the community; she restored order by making it clear that admission to prayer meetings would be refused to those who brought personal criticism into public prayer.

There was also trouble over dancing. Shaw enjoyed dancing and had no personal objection to it; however, the rules of the church positively prohibited it, and she considered it her duty to uphold the rules. One of those who supported dancing was the influential father of Shaw's former friend, Mrs. Addey. Nevertheless, Shaw stood firm on the principle that an established regulation must be observed, offering to resign if necessary. Again she was successful in taking a firm stand and refusing to be intimidated by anyone.

Soon she had an additional parish, located three miles from East Dennis. Here she held weekly services on Sunday afternoons.

Although a licensed preacher and a graduate in theology, Shaw was not ordained. This meant that she could not administer the sacraments, nor baptize, nor receive members into her church. She was permitted to perform the marriage service and to bury the dead. Her application for ordination to the New England Spring Conference of the Methodist Episcopal Church held in Boston in 1880 was refused. The General Conference concurred in this and took the additional step of revoking her license to preach. She then applied to the Methodist Protestant Church at the conference held in Tarrytown, New York, in October 1880. After considerable discussion, a large majority voted for her ordination.

Shaw entered Boston University's School of Medicine in 1882, graduating three years later. (This was 35 years after Elizabeth Blackwell entered medical school under more difficult circumstances.) Her church congregations permitted her to be in Boston certain days of the week, and she was apparently able to carry on satisfactorily as a minister while studying medicine. Curiously, she had no intention of practicing — she merely wished to gain a certain amount of medical knowledge, and was urged on by James, now a physician. Her salary enabled her to help her parents and afforded her a comfortable living.

Courses in theology and medicine and the experiences that accompanied them widened Shaw's horizons. She realized that contemporary women were fighting great battles for suffrage, for temperance, for social purity, "and in every word they uttered, I heard a rallying-cry," she would note. She saw women overworked and underpaid, as they competed with men in industry. She could find only one solution to the injustice — the enfranchisement of women. So in 1885, she resigned her pastorates to become part of the suffrage movement — to her, a great cause. Her new position was lecturer and organizer of the Massachusetts Woman Suffrage Association, presided over by Lucy Stone.

Years before, in 1848, the first women's rights convention in the United States was held at Seneca Falls, New York, with more than 250 women and some 40 men present. There was a call for votes for women, and the idea began to take form. The movement suffered a setback 20 years later when the 15th Amendment to the Constitution gave Negro males the right to vote (but failed to include women). In 1869, Susan B. Anthony and Elizabeth Cady Stanton formed the National Woman's Suffrage Association to gain the vote by congressional amendment; this organization also addressed other women's issues. In 1878, the Susan B. Anthony Amendment, which would become the 19th Amendment, was formally introduced. It would continue to be introduced until 1918. When

Shaw joined the suffrage movement, only the territory of Wyoming had granted full voting rights to women.

She soon became acquainted with various notables devoted to suffrage (and other liberal causes), among them John Greenleaf Whittier; Louisa May Alcott and Bronson, her father; William Lloyd Garrison; Theodore Weld; Wendell Phillips; the Emersons; and Julie Ward Howe. Shaw knew temperance leader Frances Willard well. With Susan B. Anthony—"the torch that illuminated my life"—she formed a strong friendship and an effective working relationship that lasted until the former's death in 1906.

For a short period, Shaw was employed by the Slaton Lecture Bureau of Chicago and later by the Redpath Bureau of Boston. She lectured throughout the country in chautauquas—presentations connected with a highly successful adult education movement—her subjects for the most part being suffrage and temperance. Travel arrangements were far from convenient, and Shaw recounted all-night journeys in freight-cars, engines and cabooses as well as 30- and 40-mile drives in blizzards and bitter cold.

Sometimes there were misunderstandings. Arriving in a town, she found herself advertised as one "who whistled before Queen Victoria" and the person scheduled to lecture on "The Missing Link." With her usual resourcefulness, Shaw requested that the audience sing a patriotic song. During that short interval, she decided on a suffrage speech, using the idea that woman was the missing link in the government of the United States.

Strenuous as life on the lecture circuit was, she seemed to thrive on it, electing to continue on it for many years. She apparently did well financially.

From 1888 to 1892, she worked as a national lecturer for the Woman's Christian Temperance Union in the suffrage department. This was an unpaid position, but she was allowed to keep her lecture earnings.

In 1890, the National Woman's Suffrage Association merged with the more conservative group known as the American Woman Suffrage Association to form the National American Woman Suffrage Association. Susan B. Anthony was its first president. Shaw was appointed the new organization's national lecturer, then its vice-president-at-large in addition to her position as lecturer.

In 1900, Carrie Chapman Catt succeeded Miss Anthony as president. Although Shaw was deeply disappointed at being passed over, she

Anna Howard Shaw, M.D.

Anna Howard Shaw in pulpit robe. Courtesy The Schlesinger Library, Radcliffe College.

graciously supported the able Mrs. Catt. The latter's resignation in 1904 brought about Shaw's tenure, which lasted 11 years.

Kraditor, a historian, noted that although Shaw devoted her truly great oratorical powers to the suffrage cause, speech making by then had lost its importance, and that deficiencies in her administrative policies caused adverse effects on the suffrage movement.

Linkugel and Solomon, communication experts, were not so critical. They pointed out that under her leadership, membership increased from 17,000 to 183,000, also that during the period when she was very active as a lecturer for suffrage (1890–1915), the following states voted for equal suffrage: Colorado, Idaho, Utah, Washington, California, Arizona, Kansas, Oregon, Nevada and Montana.

With the collaboration of Elizabeth Jordan, Shaw wrote her autobiography. *The Story of a Pioneer* was published in 1915.

When the United States became embroiled in World War I, Shaw, a steadfast pacifist, served as chairman of the Woman's Committee of the Council of National Defense. For this work, she was awarded in 1919 the Distinguished Service Medal, the first living American woman so honored.

At the age of 72, she had an opportunity to work for peace. William Howard Taft, the ex-president, and Abbott Lawrence Lowell, president of Harvard University, invited "the foremost leader of woman suffrage" to accompany them on a lecture tour to rally support for President Wilson's peace plan, especially the League of Nations part of the treaty. The tour involved 14 states from New Hampshire to Kansas. Shaw worked very hard, sometimes speaking four or five times a day, and received great acclamation. She collapsed in Springfield, Illinois, with a temperature of 104 degrees. Her illness was diagnosed as pneumonia and inflammation of the liver. She died at her home on July 2, 1919, before the 19th Amendment to the Constitution was ratified in 1920.

Her own words make it clear that she was satisfied with her life: "Nothing bigger can come to a human being than to love a great Cause more than life itself, and to have the privilege throughout life of working for that Cause."

A 1994 publication by Wil Linkugel and Martha Solomon, *Anna Howard Shaw: Suffrage Orator and Social Reformer*, is number ten of a series on great American orators. (Some of the other nine titles dealt with the orations of Daniel Webster, Henry Ward Beecher, Edward Everett and Patrick Henry.) This excellent book pointed out that although the topics of Shaw's lectures did not always have appeal, she impressed her audiences even in an era when good speakers were numerous. These authors analyzed some of the reasons for this.

Although her physical appearance was not impressive, her carriage and demeanor conveyed dignity and authority. (Shaw was of medium height, inclined to be plump. She had brown eyes and brown hair that turned gray prematurely.) Her spirit and energy evoked such words as "grit" and "spunk" and "pluck."

Her delivery was animated, and one Kansas journalist noted that she thoroughly understood the art of gesticulation. She preferred to speak extemporaneously and seldom used notes. (She found writing difficult and stated that she needed the influence of listeners — real or fancied.) Various references have established that she could project her voice to back rows and highest galleries in great auditoriums such as the New York Hippodrome and the Albert Hall in London. Another asset was her sense of humor. As to style, Linkugel and Solomon concluded that she expressed her ideas forthrightly and simply, without resorting to bombast or elaborate language. Early in her career she learned to keep cool in the face of small disasters, interruptions, annoyances, and to continue without fluster. All these qualities led *The Morning Oregonian* on June 29, 1905, to declare: "Dr. Shaw is easily the best and foremost woman speaker in the world."

Some samples of her oratory follow.

> When a committee appealed to Congress, asking that when the Negroes were enfranchised the loyal women might share their freedom, Congress answered: "It is the negro's hour, women must wait." The Negro's house struck, again women asked for liberty, and were again assured that Congress had mightier measures to consume its time and attention — it had the South to reconstruct, and the North to bring back to a sound business basis. The severest form of punishment it could devise for the crime of treason was disfranchisement, reducing traitors to the level of loyal women, who had given all they had for their country, and this is the only recognition that Congress has ever granted them.
>
> — From a lecture delivered hundreds of times over several decades.

> I have always wanted to be a policeman and I have applied to be appointed policeman and the very first question that was asked me was, "Could you knock a man down and take him to jail?" This is some people's idea of the highest service that a policeman can render a community. Knock somebody down and take him to

jail. My idea is not so much to arrest criminals as it is to prevent crime. That is what is needed in the police force of every community. When I lived for three years in the back alleys of Boston, I saw there that it was needed to prevent crime and from that day to this I believe there is no great public gathering of any sort where we do not need women on the police force; we need them at every moving picture show, every dance house, every restaurant, every hotel and every great store with a great bargain counter and every park and every resort where the vampires who fatten on the crimes and vices of men and women gather. We need women on the police force and we will have them there some day.

—June 21, 1915

Now, all that is meant by the woman-suffrage movement lies in that first divine utterance to man: "It is not good for man to stand alone"—either in the home, or the state, or even in the Garden of Eden. Therefore, we women are asking that the word "male" be stricken out of our State and National Constitutions, and that these shall read as they ought to have read in the beginning: Every citizen, twenty-one years of age, possessing the necessary qualifications may cast one vote at every election and have that vote counted. That is all suffragists are asking. And yet, by the opposition with which we are met and the horror of the anti-suffragists, one might suppose that we were seeking to up-root the foundations of the government, that we were asking that women would leave their homes and forsake their children, should cease to love their husbands, and should become so absorbed in politics that they would never again think of anything else in the world; whereas all we are asking of men is to be true to the fundamental principles of democracy, and to take, in their day, the step that belongs to their time, as their ancestors in their day took the steps which belonged to their time, in the evolution of a republic out of a monarchy. We are not yet fully evolved; there is one step still to be taken; and no State as a part nor the United States as a whole can become a republic until the word "male" is stricken out of their respective constitution and the word "citizen" incorporated; until all citizens are alike free.

— From a speech stenographically recorded and then printed as a pamphlet.

Skill in public speaking has always been part of American culture. Anna Howard Shaw possessed that skill in a high degree and used it on behalf of a great reform.

Mother Cabrini

Francesca Cabrini was a human dynamo, although she was in ill health for much of her life. She got things done — no matter the difficulties encountered — because she sincerely believed that Jesus Christ intended her to take certain actions. These included the founding of an order of nuns to help the poor, and the founding of orphanages and schools and hospitals where they were needed. A devout woman and believer in mysticism, she was a good combination of a Martha and a Mary.

On July 15, 1850, Agostino Cabrini and Stella (Oldini) Cabrini became the parents of their tenth child, born two months early. The small, frail baby was christened Maria Francesca, but known to her family as Cecchina. The Cabrinis lived in Sant' Angelo, which was about 20 miles from Milan, Italy. Agostino, a pious Roman Catholic, was a prosperous farmer. (His cousin Agostino Depretis would become prime minister of Italy in 1876.) Agostino's wife was also religious and the sister of a priest who was noted for his concern for the poor. Their children were Francesca, Rosa, a daughter who was mentally deficient and three sons. As Francesca grew older, Rosa, 15 years her senior, became almost a second mother to the blond, blue-eyed child.

Francesca was brought up in an atmosphere of family love. She received her first communion when she was 9. By the time she was 13, she wanted to be a missionary, prompted perhaps by hearing read aloud at home *Annals of the Propagation of the Faith*, a missionary magazine. Also, a missionary priest who preached at Sant' Angelo gave Francesca inspiration.

She lived through tempestuous times: Italy was unified in 1861, while nine years later, the temporal power of the Pope ended. Francesca's early education was supervised at school and at home by Rosa, who had become a certified teacher. Rosa had high standards and was demanding in various ways. At 13, Francesca was sent to Arluno to the boarding school run by the Daughters of the Sacred Heart. She was to be trained for the teaching profession. Five years later, in 1868, she took examinations at Lodi that entitled her to a teaching diploma.

The next year, Agostino died suddenly, and 11 months later, so did Stella. Rosa, Francesca and the handicapped daughter remained in the family home. When smallpox broke out early in the 1870s, Francesca contracted it after visiting infected homes. Rosa nursed her back to health; fortunately the disease caused no disfigurement.

The two sisters had received their teaching diplomas under Austrian auspices; now the Italian government ordered that all those holding teaching certificates be recertified under the Italian government. The Cabrini daughters attended refresher courses at Lodi, later passing the required tests.

Soon after Francesca's recovery from smallpox, the local parish priest asked her to substitute for two weeks for a sick teacher at a school in nearby Vidardo. This she did, but the tenure turned out to be two years, during which time she proved herself a highly successful and well-liked teacher. She also came to know well a priest there named Don Antonio Serrati.

At 23 she was bent on becoming a nun, and applied for admission to the Daughters of the Sacred Heart, the order that had educated her. She was refused because of poor health. Cabrini then approached the Canossan Sisters at Crema, but found that Don Serrati, as well as two priests from Sant' Angelo, were opposed to her taking the veil. Cabrini accepted the refusal as the divine will of God. She truly desired to be a missionary and was convinced that her day would come. At the same time, she was obedient to what she believed was the command of Christ. Throughout her life she would practice this type of obedience and would expect it of her sisters.

Don Serrati soon became monsignor and was appointed provost of the parish church of Codogno, where a small private orphanage called the House of Providence was located. Founded five years previously, the orphanage was in financial straits and in need of reorganization in 1874. Antonia Tondini, who was eccentric and difficult, ran the home with the help of her similarly dispositioned associate, Teresa Calza, and a pious woman named Maria Giuseppa Alberici. Besides orphans, the house had a small group of religious women who carried on various good works. The women wore religious garb but had not taken vows. The Bishop of Lodi, under whose jurisdiction the House of Providence came, put a former Sant' Angelo priest in charge of the operation, expecting improvements. The cleric recommended that convent methods be used to run the institution, and suggested that Cabrini take over. He had been impressed with her performance at Vidard and was aware of her desire to be a religious.

Cabrini was persuaded to go to Codogno, fully realizing that she would be in a most difficult position. Naturally Tondini resented Cabrini, ignoring her for the most part.

Cabrini gradually brought about improvement; various educational programs for both youth and adults were instituted; there were even recreational opportunities for working girls; and more young women entered the Sisters of Providence. Cabrini found that six or so of the sisters, like herself, desired to live a real religious life. In 1877, she and seven of them professed their first vows. At that time, the bishop formally appointed her Superior of the House of Providence, an act that increased Tondini's ire.

With regard to the Cabrini family, the impaired sister, Maddalena, lived until 1895, cared for by Rosa. Rosa then sailed for Argentina to join her brother, who had emigrated previously. The others died at an early age. Tragically, Rosa contracted a fatal illness and died soon after arriving in South America.

Francesca's tenure at Codogno lasted for six years. Frustrating as it was, she regarded it as a probation for the missionary work that she believed would come. Finally the bishop closed the house, following a lawsuit by Tondini and Calza against the diocese. (They had ceded land to the diocese for the orphanage.) Remembering Cabrini's desire to be a missionary, he counseled her to found an institute for missionary sisters.

Monsignor Serrati supplied some money and a house. The latter did not suit Cabrini, but she found what had once been a Franciscan monastery — and in good repair. There were almost no furnishings, no lights, and so on. In the chapel, a picture of the Sacred Heart was installed above the altar. In each of the 66 additional houses that she would found, a picture of the Sacred Heart of Jesus was hung above the altar. This was because the order's title was Institute of the Missionary Sisters of the Sacred Heart of Jesus, Cabrini's contention being that the institute "came forth from the Heart of Jesus."

She chose for the motto of the Institute "For the greater glory of the most Sacred Heart of Jesus." The principal patrons were St. Francis Xavier and St. Francis de Sales. Her own religious name was Mother

Mother Francesca Saveria Cabrini

Courtesy Catholic Health Partners.

Francesca Saveria Cabrini. The rule of life she wrote for her missionary sisters was approved by the bishop in 1881. There was some dissent about the use of "Missionary" in the title; missionaries of that day were men, not women. But in the end, Cabrini had her way. The habit chosen was black; a distinctive checkered veil and lace edged headcap, bow at the chin, a cincture fringed with macramé and a simple silver cross identified the sisters. Papal approval would come later.

From this unusual beginning came an international order of nuns that would bring solace to immigrant Italians in public hospitals where their language was not understood. They would also go to those with deadly yellow fever, to those in prisons, some awaiting execution, to Italians on cotton plantations, in mines, on fishing boats — there were few barriers to where her "daughters" would go. These women would run orphanages, schools and hospitals — all dedicated to serve, for the most part, needy Italians.

One of Cabrini's strengths was the selection of excellent young women for her order. She highly valued humility and simplicity. She was demanding, yet loving, but did not expect of subordinates what she would not do herself. Her charismatic personality inspired them to reach great heights. Despite the fact that she continuously set almost impossible goals, these goals were accomplished through the faith and steadfastness of a band of loyal followers.

There were critics. In the early part of this century, some members of her order complained to the Vatican that Cabrini was tyrannical. The matter came up again in the 1930s prior to her beatification. In addition, the two chief instigators of the criticism implied that the superior general who succeeded Cabrini was really her daughter. Poor character references discredited the testimony of the women who had advanced the accusations.

The Bishop of Lodi defined the function of Cabrini's institute as religious work and the care of youth to be carried out through the establishment of schools and orphanages. The new order had to generate money to exist, so a paying school as well as an orphanage was instituted. (It would be thus in some other enterprises in which Cabrini was involved; to finance schools and hospitals, the more affluent sometimes had to contribute to the care of the poor.) The school had a chance of success because at the time, there was an anticlerical atmosphere in Italy, and some Catholic families welcomed the opportunity to have their daughters educated under church auspices.

The Codogno Institute attracted orphans (some from the House of Providence) as well as day students and boarders; others came to learn embroidery or cooking; many desired religious instructions. Financing the operation was a constant struggle, but it did not overwhelm the Mother Superior. For believers, there are stories of miraculous appearances of money and food where there had been none before.

There are few details about Cabrini's health, but apparently it was precarious, even at this stage of her career. Malaria is mentioned as one disease that threatened her. She was of small stature, which probably gave an impression of frailty. On the other hand, references to her piercing glance gave no impression of sickliness.

After founding several additional houses, Cabrini set her sights on Rome, where she traveled in 1887. After many difficulties, she was granted papal permission to found two houses in the Eternal City.

She journeyed to Rome again in December 1888, for an audience with Pope Leo XIII. At that time, her institute numbered 105 sisters and 40 novices. For a second audience, she had her heart set on going to China but was commanded by the Holy Father to go "not to the east, but to the West!"

The West referred to the United States, to which hundreds of thousands of Italians — some close to starvation — were emigrating. Southern Italy, dependent on agriculture, was in economic straits due to a variety of factors; malaria was a serious health threat; employment opportunities were few; political corruption was common. By 1887, the government was encouraging people to leave — and leave they did for America at an annual rate of some quarter of a million. Most of them came from central and southern Italy.

America was not El Dorado. Many of the immigrants were illiterate; many were exploited, working under substandard conditions for a pittance. They usually lived in crowded slums. In contrast to the Irish and German immigrants, the Italians were less respected; in company with most foreigners, they were heartily disliked by natives because they would work for lower wages than American laborers. Another point of contention was that many Italians hoped to return home after amassing sufficient money. They had little contact with the Catholic Church, mainly because there was a lack of priests who spoke Italian. (In Italy, there was one priest to about 370 persons; as late as 1899, Chicago had only one priest to about 7,500 Italians.) One immigrant to the United States wrote back to his homeland, "Here we live like animals; one lives and dies without a priest, without teachers and without doctors."

Having visited this country, Monsignor Giovanni Battista Scalabrini,

Bishop of Piacenza, was aware of the problems his countrymen were facing. In his pamphlet, *Italian Emigration to America,* he had written:

> I see these poor Italian immigrants in a foreign land, among people who do not speak their language, easily falling prey to cruel exploitation ... fatigued, sick, sighing in vain for their quaint and humble little towns in Italy, and finally dying without the consolation of their dearest ones, without the enlivening words of faith which hold out to them the reward the Lord has promised to the good and the unfortunate.

Scalabrini had urged Cabrini to introduce her order to the United States. He believed that the presence of her sisters would do much to alleviate the conditions he described. Cabrini had not been convinced until the pope spoke.

With six of her nuns, Cabrini set sail from Le Havre for New York on March 23, 1889. This was the first of numerous sea voyages for the Mother Superior — passage was often a reduced fare for religious purposes. Although Archbishop Michael Augustine Corrigan of New York City had previously promised an Italian children's orphanage that would serve as a convent, it had not materialized. A letter stating so had arrived after the nuns' departure. Now the archbishop suggested that they return to Europe.

Cabrini's response was that they were in the country by order of the Holy See and that they intended to stay. On May 8, the first two orphans arrived to live in the convent-orphanage that had been founded. This was the first of many that would follow. There would be orphans from a yellow fever epidemic; orphans of the eruption of Mt. Etna; orphans of an earthquake in Sicily; orphans of mining disasters, orphans of World War I and of other catastrophes. Abandoned children and some whose parent or parents were unable to care for them were also accepted.

A day school with 200 children was soon in operation in an Italian church. Many more schools would also follow. A trained teacher, Cabrini realized the value of her own religious education. She would write: "Fashion the hearts of the students to a love of religion and the practice of virtue." She contended that the greatest heritage of a girl is a good education.

The nuns systematically visited all the families in Little Italy. Living under appalling conditions, these people were delighted to be addressed in their native tongue. (Cabrini herself found difficulty in learning English and spoke it with a strong foreign accent.) A newspaper article mentioned refined and delicate women "climbing up narrow, steep stairs, going down into foul cellers, and entering certain dens into which not even a policeman would venture unaccompanied."

Temporary quarters for both convent and school were secured. Bishop Corrigan had limited Cabrini's fundraising to Italians. This posed a problem; few could pay school tuition, so that was not a source of income. In addition, most Italians had little cash to spare, so fundraising among them was not very fruitful. Fortunately, other orders of nuns provided some assistance and cooperation. However, beginning in this period, the Missionary Sisters of the Sacred Heart were forced to beg for the livelihood of those entrusted to their care.

Cabrini was needed in Italy, so she returned there in July. This pattern of organizing, delegating and leaving characterized her activities for the rest of her life. She appears to have had superior ability to organize, and with this gift, a personality that made people receptive to her ideas. How she financed her many operations is difficult to understand, because most of the time she had little more than faith.

It should be understood that while Cabrini's aim was to bring the love of Christ to others, she was not the product of an ecumenical era. She definitely proselytized for the Catholic faith, and she had little patience for anyone who challenged traditional Catholic teaching.

She set sail for New York in April 1890, bringing with her more sisters. Her immediate concern was an excellent property owned by the Jesuits high above the Hudson River known as West Park. Its one negative aspect was lack of water on the site. However, when Cabrini ordered a digging at a spot that was never dry, a good spring was discovered. Aware that she needed a permanent home for her sisters, the Jesuits made her a good offer, which she accepted. The orphanage was moved from Manhattan to West Park, becoming the first U.S. motherhouse of the order and the novitiate for this country.

From the beginning, Cabrini showed unusual business acumen. Over the years, she was involved in numerous real estate transactions as she started new enterprises and extended existing ones. Not only did she have exceptional judgment about property, but she also drove a hard bargain.

Cabrini spent the latter half of 1890 and the first part of 1891 in Italy, expanding the order's operations. She returned to North America because there was a call for the order to take over an orphanage in

Granada and to open a boarding school for girls. Life was hard in Nicaragua due to revolutions, epidemics, earthquakes and torrid weather, but she fulfilled the request.

Because Archbishop Francis Janssens of New Orleans wanted religious subjects to care for Italians in that city, Cabrini made it her destination in March 1892. She had recently had a bad attack of malaria, contracted in Nicaragua, and she never fully recovered from the infection. Despite this chronic illness, she carried on with great energy. In New Orleans there was unusual hatred of Cabrini's countrymen. This had manifested itself in lynchings. Nevertheless, the foundation that she brought to that city proved a great success. Years later, her sisters there would be remembered for their heroic behavior during devastating yellow fever epidemics.

Before her death in Chicago in 1917, Cabrini established 67 houses in Italy, the United States, Nicaragua, Argentina, France, Spain, England and Brazil. She continued to found orphanages and schools. In 1899 many schools were started in or near New York City for poor Italian children. Many Italians worked in mining and agriculture in Colorado, California and Washington; she also turned her attention to these areas. For example, in 1902, Cabrini went to Denver to found a school. Many of the operations begun soon expanded and needed new facilities.

In all situations, the sisters were there to lend comfort and to express the love of Christ. Although the original sisters were Italian, when Cabrini died, a quarter of her "daughters" in the United States were non–Italian.

The order's first hospital was established in New York in 1892. The priests sent by Bishop Scalabrini had started a small operation for Italians, but it had not been a financial success. When they requested Cabrini to take over, she was not willing to assume debts or work under the fathers. Then she had a dream in which she was reproached for her attitude by Mary, mother of Jesus. The experience prompted her to assume the responsibility. Incidentally, Cabrini frequently had dreams that influenced her decisions. Whether due to shrewd inferences or compelling dreams, her decisions were, for the most part, good.

As to the situation at hand, 25 patients needed care. Cabrini sent 15 to other hospitals, keeping 10 who particularly objected to being moved. Of the latter, a few were dying. Renting new quarters, she placed those under her charge in what she named Columbus Hospital, in honor of the 400th anniversary of Columbus' discovery of America. From very frugal beginnings, this hospital grew to become one of the city's respected institutions. Gifts and money poured in; skilled doctors donated their services. Italians who did not speak English were grateful to find themselves understood. They were also delighted to receive familiar food.

A few years later, two sailors from an Italian war ship in port contracted typhoid fever. Refused by a Protestant establishment, they were admitted to Columbus Hospital. When one died and was buried from the chapel, the consul-general for Italy attended the funeral. The upshot was that for a small fee, all sick sailors on Italian ships in the port of New York would in the future be received at Columbus Hospital. Soon the building of the former Clinic and Post-Graduate Hospital of New York was purchased for use, and by 1895 was legally incorporated by the State of New York. Over the years, there were changes and enlargements; at the time of her death, Cabrini had drawn up plans for a new structure.

At the request of Archbishop Quigley of Chicago, another Columbus Hospital was founded there in 1905. With many private patients, it very soon became self-sufficient. By 1916, a third Columbus Hospital had been established in Seattle.

Twenty-five years after the founding of the Missionary Sisters of the Sacred Heart of Jesus, 100,000 patients had been treated in Columbus Hospitals. Countless orphans and pupils had grown to womanhood under the aegis of the order. By 1917, the year Cabrini died, the great waves of Italian immigrants to the United States had subsided; Italians were well integrated into the population.

Cabrini became a naturalized U.S. citizen in 1909. She had hoped to retire at age 60, but was urged to stay on by her "daughters" from all over the world. She died in 1917 in Chicago at the age of 67.

The first U.S. citizen to attain sainthood, Maria Francesca Cabrini was canonized by Pope Pius XII in 1946.

It is obvious that Mother Cabrini possessed unusual abilities that she was able to use in an era when the U.S. Italian immigrant population was growing at an exceptional rate. Some of her ideas would be unacceptable today. To exemplify, in Nicaragua she denied a child of illegitimate birth admission to her school. Although done to emphasize high moral standards, it would currently be considered discriminatory and unfair to an innocent person.

In many ways, Mother Cabrini was ahead of her times. Her leadership qualities and independence of the hierarchy were not often seen in a woman. In education she frowned on denigrating students and corporal punishment; she realized the importance of self-esteem and endeavored to provide a good atmosphere for teaching. Believing that Italians should preserve their cultural heritage, she promoted the learning of the Italian language. In contrast, most immigrants were urged to become Americanized as quickly as possible, and many forgot or declined to learn the language of their parents. Classes in her schools were conducted in English, so the language of the adopted country was not neglected. Perhaps influenced by visiting prisoners, she was against capital punishment.

Whatever her sentiments, Mother Cabrini touched and improved the lives of thousands of her countrymen. Today the Missionary Sisters of the Sacred Heart, along with dedicated lay workers, carry on her work in ways that suit the times. They are active in many foreign countries, most recently in Taiwan, the Philippines and Russia. In the United States, their work embraces many of the areas that concerned their foundress. But it has adapted to the needs at hand; today's ministry to immigrants and refugees is involved with few Italians. In addition to instruction at the elementary and secondary school level, the order now offers higher education. Surely Mother Cabrini would be proud of her modern "daughters."

Mary Adelaide Nutting

Florence Nightingale, by her work in the Crimean War, had made nursing a respected profession. Yet in 1889, the year that Canadian Mary Adelaide Nutting entered the first class to graduate from the Johns Hopkins Training School for Nurses, the students served long hours at repetitive tasks and work that could well have been done by untrained individuals. These students had had little preparation for the clinical situations to which they were assigned. Nutting did much to change this; using the methods of professional education, she advanced the status of nursing. "Compassion may provide the motive but knowledge is our only working power," she once said.

Mary Adelaide was the fifth child of Vespasion and Harriet (Peasley) Nutting. She was born on November 1, 1858, in Frost Village, Quebec. An older baby sister had died; a younger one would survive. Vespasion had Loyalist forebearers. (The United Empire Loyalists were settlers that remained faithful to the British cause during and after the American Revolution. They migrated from the 13 colonies to Canada, mainly to Nova Scotia and Quebec.) Vespasion had learned the shoe-making trade, but did not earn enough to provide well for his family. The situation grew worse as manufactured shoes increased in popularity. Harriet did much to support the family with her needlework, in which she was skilled, and her millinery. In contrast to her husband, she was ambitious and intended a better lot for her children.

After seven years in Frost Village, Harriet decided to move the Nuttings to nearby Waterloo in 1861, where there would be more advantages. She found a job for her husband, but it was not lucrative; she was busier than ever with her needle. Addie, as her daughter was called, soon had a baby sister named Armine, whom she mothered. Vespasion's garden, along with what he provided by fishing and hunting, ensured that his family was never hungry, however shabby their clothes.

Adelaide attended the local academy. At 15 she was sent to a convent close to home to study French and music. She was also enrolled for a short time at a private school in Montreal that emphasized social accomplishments, voice, piano and the like. Later she went to Lowell, Massachusetts, to live with relatives. Here she studied design and had private music lessons. Her early aspirations were towards a serious career in music, but there was little money for that. Her oldest brother had graduated in law, but the family could not become too dependent on him, although they were a closely knit group.

Returning home from Lowell, Adelaide helped her mother with sewing for the next three years. A hired girl did the household chores to give the women more time and energy for remunerative work. Adelaide did not care for Waterloo. In 1903, she would write to Armine that an unfathomable, irresistible gloom always settled on her there. She described it then as the place where their mother had worked and suffered and where Adelaide and Armine had lived out their sordid and miserable childhood.

One of the Nutting sons was employed by the postal department in Ottawa. Harriet used this as an opportunity to get Adelaide, now 23, and Armine, now 20, to Ottawa, where they might meet promising future husbands. The plan was to rent the Nutting home in Waterloo and to send the furniture to Ottawa to use in a rented flat where they could all live together. There was hope that Adelaide could give music lessons and that Armine could teach elocution.

Vespasion refused to go. He was happy in Waterloo with his dog, his low-paying job and directing the Methodist choir. His son and daughter-in-law offered him a room in their home, an offer he accepted. The correspondence between Ottawa and Waterloo has been preserved (as well as many other family letters), and it is clear that there was close communication between Vespasion and his absent family. He sent what money he could.

Life in Canada's capital was certainly more interesting than in Waterloo. Adelaide had some social life, even suitors; she found one music pupil. Her sister took a teaching position in Newfoundland; eventually marriage would make it her home.

In 1884, Harriet Nutting died. Adelaide remained in Ottawa to keep house for her brother. Although she had given up hope for a professional career in music, her mezzo-soprano voice was heard at church and some musical affairs. She made a little money by copying records for a government office.

The next year, her Ottawa brother got married. Invited to visit a cousin in Lowell, Massachusetts, for the winter, Adelaide accepted. During that time, she talked to her cousin about becoming a nurse; her mother's illness had brought home to her how little she knew about sickness.

She became familiar with the work of Florence Nightingale. Nursing seemed attractive; she could enroll in a hospital training school and receive board, lodging and a small stipend. She was close to 30, and needed to think about her future. Although she had had offers of marriage and had been engaged twice, she thought matrimony unlikely for her. (She wrote her sister in 1894 that she knew she would make a husband the most miserable being on earth four days out of the seven.) She was interested in the training school of a new hospital under the auspices of the Johns Hopkins University in Baltimore. An added attraction was the presence of Canadians on the staff: Drs. William Osler and Henri Lafleur and Miss Isabel Hampton. The latter was principal of the Training School for Nurses.

Nutting began her training on November 1, 1889, as one of 14 probationers. They were a mixed bag. One, like Nutting, had specialized in music; one had a master's degree in classics; one was a 35-year-old widow with five children; one was educated in Germany, spoke only limited English and some French. The school had formally opened on October 9. The student nurses were required to be available from 7 A.M. to 9 P.M. with an hour off for lunch, rest and study. Most of the time they had ward duty. From 8 to 9 in the evening there might be lectures by doctors. (Between November 1 and June 26 there were 66 such lectures, delivered by 13 physicians.) Twice a week, Hampton taught classes from 5 until 6 P.M. Clara Weeks' *A Textbook of Nursing for the Use of Training Schools, Families and Private Students* had been published in 1885, and excerpts from it were dictated to probationers. There was no library since the Hopkins school operated on a tight budget. (When Nutting received her first monthly stipend of $8, she bought her own copy of the Weeks text.) A pervasive militaristic atmosphere could probably have been traced to Florence Nightingale's connection with the British Army.

In 1890, as part of nurses' training at Hopkins, a cooking school was organized under the direction of a graduate of the famous Boston Cooking School. The students were taught to prepare items that patients might require.

Nutting made a good impression on Hampton, a Bellevue Hospital graduate. A lifelong friendship developed between them, and it is clear that Hampton influenced Nutting's professional career.

The first year of training flew by. Nutting had done well and was enjoying her new life. After a short vacation, she was ready to start the second and final year.

Most babies were still being delivered at home, so nurses were trained to work in that setting. The second-year students were sent into houses to do private nursing. Hampton objected to the latter practice. The students lived in the family home and the hours worked were excessive, but her main criticisms were that the students were unduly subjected to contagion and that they were unsupervised. Hampton personally favored a visiting or public nursing program for her students.

Nutting encountered a case of typhoid fever when she did her four-month stint of private duty nursing. Her write-up of the case brought her a prize and publication in the *Trained Nurse and Hospital Review* of March 1891.

That year Hampton formed a journal club for Hopkins nurses. Lavinia Dock, a Bellevue graduate who was a nursing instructor at Hopkins, would soon write *Materia Medica* for nurses; Mary Boland, the dietetics instructor, was in the process of writing *A Handbook of Invalid Cookery*; Hampton was making plans for her *Nursing: Its Principle and Practices*. Such a climate undoubtedly made its impression on Nutting; she realized that nursing had ramifications beyond the bedside.

On graduation day, Nutting heard Dr. Osler tell her classmates:

> You will be better women for the life that you have led here, better women in that the eyes of your souls have been opened, the range of your sympathies has been ordered, and your classmates have been molded by the events in which you have participated during the past two years.

Hampton intended, when possible, to place her graduates in positions of responsibility at Hopkins. Nutting's first position was that of head nurse on Dr. Osler's ward. When Hampton resigned to marry Dr. Hunter Robb, she recommended Nutting as her successor.

The trustees appointed Nutting to an "acting" position at a salary of $900 a year, which was $300 less than they had paid Hampton. The temporary appointee took over the supervision of 13 head nurses, 24 senior student nurses, 36 junior nurses and a diet kitchen teacher.

In December 1894, Nutting was appointed superintendent of

nurses and principal of the training school, effective September 1, 1895, at a salary of $1,200. In the interim, she took a leave of absence to visit hospitals in the United States and Great Britain. It was arranged that a Hopkins graduate, class of '92, would take over in her absence.

Nutting returned to her alma mater in September, intending to institute three changes — none of which was an original idea with her. She advocated a three-year curriculum, a reduction in the student's working day to eight hours and the abolition of student stipends, with the money used to improve educational facilities. "Are pupil nurses to be reduced to servitude?" she asked. She called for less work and more education. Her ideas reached receptive ears and the trustees decided to study the matter.

When the American Society of Superintendents of Training Schools for Nurses met in February 1896, in Philadelphia, Nutting spoke on hours of duty. She had statistics from many training schools. From the 111 hospitals responding to her query, working hours varied from 15½ to 17 in most.

It was through national meetings like this that Nutting gained fame in her profession. She made careful studies, summarized data and presented her materials concisely. Much of the work was done by committees between meetings, and she would be a member of many of these committees (as well as holding office). She was very interested in the organization of nurses, and through the society would work on many issues. The Society of Superintendents became the National League for Nursing (NLN).

Soon word was received that the trustees had adopted the plan she submitted. This was a good beginning. There would be many more innovations — for example, the introduction of industrial, visiting and school nursing. She believed that a student nurse should have pertinent theoretical knowledge before being exposed to the wards, as she had been. Realizing that it would take time to convince the powers that be that hers was a more reasonable approach, she bided her time. She had great expectations for students, who considered her aloof but fair. The doctors backed up her policies. Her school became a model, adding to her sense of responsibility. She worked extremely hard, sometimes beyond her powers of endurance. Vacations with family members helped her to relax and to forget the ever-pressing professional matters before her.

By 1898, Nutting and Isabel Hampton Robb were working on "A Possible Course at Teachers College for a Training Class for Administrative Positions in Nursing." Robb, who had retained her interest in nursing, frequented national meetings and was still a popular figure in the profession. The two women were sure that nursing would benefit from the approach used by Teachers College of Columbia University. Dean James Earl Russell was sufficiently impressed with their curriculum to offer it as an advanced course for trained nurses under the title of "Hospital Economics." It would be under the administration of the woman who directed the training of home economics teachers.

With the Society of Superintendents providing some financial aid, two nurses began an eight-month study at Teachers College. This included psychology, biology, domestic science, physical science and special lectures in subjects dealing with nursing education. The candidate would then spend three to five months at private duty nursing. The following year, six students enrolled, but there were some complaints about the course offerings. As an example, the students believed that psychology should be eliminated. (Dean Russell would not permit this, but the instructor in the course was told to take into account the interests and limitations of the nursing students.)

The Nurses Associated Alumnae of the United States and Canada (ultimately the American Nursing Association) was another organization that held annual meetings for graduate nurses. In October 1900, it published the first issue of the *American Journal of Nursing*. Nutting was one of the original stockholders in the enterprise and worked hard to obtain subscribers. She would be a contributor for many years.

In April 1902, Nutting took an enforced vacation because of a breakdown. After extensive travel in Europe and visits to Newfoundland, she returned to Baltimore in September. She and Armine Gosling, the sister whom she had mothered years ago, had remained close, and she always enjoyed stays with the Goslings, who lived in St. John's. Through them she came to know well Dr. Wilfred Grenfell, the English physician and missionary who was famous for his work among Labrador fishermen.

States were slowly passing nurse registration laws. At the 1904 meeting of the Maryland State Association of Graduate Nurses, Nutting, as its president, noted that during the organization's first year a nurse registration law had materialized in their state. This meant that all nurses practicing in Maryland would be subject to examination and required to pay a fee. She now urged a central directory for nurses and promoted the concept of school nurses.

Another project occupying Nutting's time was writing a history of nursing. Her collaborator was nurse and feminist Lavinia Dock.

In December 1905, Nutting realized that her constitution could no longer keep up the pace she had set for herself. In 1904, for example, she had published no less than eight articles in nursing publications. She had spent the last 14 years in charge of the Hopkins hospital services and its training school for nurses. By combining innovation and good judgment she had made it an exemplary institution. She had even succeeded in introducing a preparatory course before ward duty — this despite the fact that it was more expensive than the old system of using student labor before the student had any theoretical understanding of what she was doing. Nutting loved Hopkins, Baltimore and the life she led; her many congenial friends; her comfortable apartment in the Nurses' Home. But the stresses were great, and it was time to leave.

A short time later, she contracted diphtheria, a serious disease. This was followed by convalescence in Atlantic City.

The hospital economics course at Teachers College now had an additional year. When Nutting was offered the opportunity to direct it, she accepted a three-year appointment as full professor at a salary of $2,500. She was granted a leave of absence without pay during 1906. Her work was to include "investigation and instruction in the management and administration of households, hospitals, asylums, dormitories and other domestic institutions."

Thus Mary Adelaide Nutting became the first nurse to hold professional rank. She had no degree, but that is unimportant. She was a well-educated woman, mainly through self-instruction. More importantly, she was an authority on nursing; she was aware of the needs of the profession and possessed sufficient vision and flexibility to institute changes as they were needed.

Before assuming her new position, Nutting went abroad from May until September 1907. She attended the International Council of Nurses in Paris; she sought material for her *History of Nursing*; she visited friends, and, as on other such occasions, enjoyed Europe's culture. The highlight of her experience was a visit to Florence Nightingale, then 87. This was especially meaningful to Nutting, who collected books, essays and articles by and about Nightingale.

On assuming her new position, one of Nutting's first acts was to arrange for her students to have contact with Henry Street Settlement, created by Lillian Wald. Wald had begun a visiting nurse service there in 1893 for immigrants in the Lower East Side. By 1907 it covered a large area of New York's slums. Nutting realized the importance and possibilities of public health nursing; another nursing organization with

Mary Adelaide Nutting

Portrait by Cecilia Beaux (1855–1942). Courtesy The Alan Chesney Medical Archives, The Johns Hopkins Medical Institutions.

which she was associated was the National Organization of Public Health Nurses.

She studied the catalogs of Teachers College, looking for courses and staff that might add relevance to her plans. For example, later on she utilized resources of the manual arts and crafts center to set up occupational therapy. Over the next four years, such courses as economics of the household, standards of living, consumer education, home finance and research methods were developed.

The first two volumes of the *History of Nursing* were published by Putnam in late fall 1907. The reviews were good. Sister Karll, founder of the German Nurses Association, arranged to translate the work into German. (The complete four-volume work was available by 1912.)

Sixteen nurses took the hospital economics course in 1908. One of them, Isabel Maitland Stewart, had trained in Winnipeg. She came to Teachers College, she said, because she wanted to teach. Nutting was impressed with her, and eventually there developed between them a relationship similar to that between Nutting herself and Isabel Hampton. Another member of the class came from Tokyo. In the years to come, the enrollment would increase significantly to include many foreign students as the hospital economics course became known nationally and internationally.

In addition to her responsibilities to Teachers College, Nutting's professional life included attendance at endless meetings, officerships in societies, committee meetings, oral presentation of papers, writing of papers and so on. She was constantly investigating new approaches and programs and often arranged for their adoption. She dreamed of autonomous nursing schools but was practical enough to realize that some time would pass before hospitals would give up their control; the economic needs of the hospital would take precedence to the educational needs of the student. Small wonder she had no time to give the suffrage cause, although she was behind it.

In 1909, an endowment of $150,000 provided for the creation of a separate Department of Nursing and Health at Teachers College.

Nutting worked very hard on a report entitled *Educational Status of Nursing* for the Office of Education. Finished in December 1911, it recorded statistics from 1,028 training schools in the United States and Puerto Rico. It was the first such comprehensive study made in the United States. At a cost of 10 cents each, many copies of the study were distributed and widely reviewed.

The year 1914 saw Nutting and two nurse friends caught in Europe when war broke out. Nutting finally got passage from Glasgow to New-foundland, thanks to her brother-in-law, Gilbert Gosling.

The 71 nurses enrolled at Teachers College that fall were told by Nutting that nursing leaders had collegiate schools as their great goal. She stressed the importance of the academic qualifications of the faculty of these schools.

The University of Minnesota already had a training school directed by a former Teachers College student. Nutting expended much effort pressing for private endowments and public funds to support training schools. She wrote speeches and articles on the subject.

With the entrance of the United States into World War I on April 6, 1917, much attention was given to the procurement of adequate nursing for the troops, at the same time ensuring satisfactory nursing care for civilians. Nutting, Lillian Wald, Lavinia Dock and other prominent nurses were against the use of short-term nurses and aides as substitutes for qualified registered nurses. Their opposition was based on the experience of British nurses who had protested unsuccessfully against socialites who were permitted to care for military personnel in serious condition.

Too old for military duty, Nutting became chairman of the National Emergency Committee on Nursing of the General Medical Council of Defence. Extensive statistical studies were done to determine the need for nurses and the potential to meet the needs. Thousands of pamphlets were written to promote recruitment to the nursing profession.

As a means of procuring more nurses, Nutting and her colleagues favored reducing the training period of college women with good scientific backgrounds. She was confident that this would provide enough well-trained nurses. She became closely associated with a project known as Vassar Camp. She convinced President McCracken that his campus, which he offered to aid the war effort, could be used to give college graduates a three-month intensive course prior to an abbreviated but complete nurses training in a good school. She designed the camp according to the plan used for concentrated officer training at Plattsburg Military Camp. Vassar Camp opened in June 1918, with 437 probationers.

Dr. William Mayo, the distinguished surgeon, was one who favored the use of aides overseas. He stated at a meeting of the Committee on Nursing with the General Medical Board that the slogan of the nurses appeared to be "The trained nurse first, God and country afterward."

An influenza epidemic that would become a pandemic struck in the fall of 1918. It was an opportunity for trainees from the Vassar Camp program to show their value. It also led Jane Delano, the national director of the American Red Cross nursing service, and an opponent to the use of aides overseas, to support the training of aides.

After the Armistice, the Committee on Nursing's Student Nurse Reserve project was turned over to the Red Cross. Nutting's final communication noted that "Thousands have entered training schools, mainly highly qualified. Some might have chosen other professions if not for the war." Of the 399 who had entered training schools after Vassar Camp, 174 graduated.

While the war was still in progress, a national committee to secure rank for military nurses had been organized with Nutting a member. President Wilson signed a bill in 1920 that did just that. The lowest rank for a qualified nurse was that of second lieutenant.

Nutting received a formal certificate that recognized her service with the Committee for Defense. It bore the seal of the United States, but was conferred on a non–American. In 1915, she had stated publicly:

> My great sympathy with American ideals, my profound belief in her principles of government have made it a delight to live among you. I hasten to add that my love for my country and race remains untouched — a vital part of my being, rooted more and more deeply as the years pass.

She also noted later: "The whole world is God's beautiful world and we are first of all his children and only in a secondary sense Americans or Canadians, or British...."

Nutting took a sabbatical year in 1921. Some of it was spent in Europe with Armine and her husband.

She resigned in 1925 at the age of 66. To her joy, her successor was Isabel Stewart. For many years Nutting took an interest in nursing affairs and was a valued adviser. She had great loyalty to the Hopkins school that had trained her, and she retained a lasting interest in it. Retirement afforded her more opportunity for reading, always one of her favorite occupations. Over time, she had assembled quite a collection of books. As she grew older, she gave thought to disposing them so that they would go where they would be appreciated. She kept in touch with her siblings and their children.

She died in 1948, at almost 90. Armine's death in 1942 had been a great blow. After that, she turned more and more to Stewart, upon whom she had long depended, both professionally and personally. The funeral was held in St. Paul's Chapel of Columbia University. According to her wishes, after cremation her ashes were buried beside her mother in Canada.

In 1922, Yale University conferred on Nutting an honorary Master of Arts degree. The citation stated: "Her devotion, courage, faith, skill and magnificent perseverance have made her today one of the most useful women in the world." Thus a Canadian woman, through her work in the United States, achieved international acclaim. The profession that she represented is now university or college based rather than hospital based, as it was in 1889 when she began her training. During the academic year 1993-94, 94,870 nursing students graduated from the following programs: baccalaureate degree — 29,912; associate degree — 58,839, diploma (hospital based)— 7,119. Currently many nurses with advanced degrees are certified in various clinical specialties.

Ernestine Schumann-Heink

Ernestine Schumann-Heink presented much of the best of German opera to the United States. Through concerts and the medium of radio, she brought beautiful music to untold numbers of Americans, both native-born citizens and those naturalized.

She was born to Hans and Charlotte (Goldman) Roessler near Prague on June 15, 1861. Her father was an Austrian army officer, her mother a well-educated woman of Hungarian-Jewish descent. Most people called her Tina. She carried memories of a youth marked by deprivation and even want, for although an Austrian army officer was allotted a piece of land to be worked, he received very little money. The family lived in barracks and made frequent moves due to Hans' transfers. Ernestine received a poor education because she was so often required to stay at home to take care of her siblings.

She remembered herself as an 11-year-old playing truant from school to visit a circus. She did odd jobs, which included cleaning monkey cages, to be fed a good meal. Another time she got some Swiss cheese that her mother fancied but could not afford by dancing and singing the Czardos, the national Hungarian dance.

At the Ursaline Convent in Prague, a mother superior predicted that her student, Tina Roessler, would become a great actress or singer. Mrs. Roessler believed in her daughter, but there was no money for the required training. Her husband was not impressed. However, a former prima donna, then married to a rich man in Prague, heard Ernestine's contralto voice at mass and was impressed. She immediately offered free voice lessons. Ernestine sang by ear, and here was an opportunity to learn to sight read. Unfortunately, the arrangement was short lived; there was a transfer to Graz.

An officer in Roessler's regiment had a daughter who had once been in opera and now gave singing lessons — Marietta von Leclair. This generous woman took over Ernestine's instruction without charge, giving her two lessons a week over an extended period. Ernestine did well, but still depended on her ear to sing and also to accompany herself on a broken down piano. Her teacher was deaf, and it was many years before Ernestine realized that she was singing louder than necessary.

At the end of two years' training, the aspiring singer attended her first opera. It was *Il Trovatore*, and Roessler was inspired by the singing of the great contralto, Marianna Brandt.

The next year, Roessler earned about $6 for singing the alto part in Beethoven's Ninth Symphony. Some of her pay was spent on secondhand white curtains to decorate her family's bare abode.

Through the kindness of friends she had an opportunity to sing for the director of the Imperial Opera in Vienna. The latter noted her homeliness and her poverty and suggested she take up dressmaking. This failure in Vienna reinforced her father's idea that his daughter should become a teacher. But Roessler had other ideas, and her mother still had faith.

Another chance came in 1875, this time to audition at the Dresden Royal Opera. A kind man made it possible for her to buy a new dress and hat and shoes. For the first time in her life, she presented a good appearance. She won a three-year contract. Her father was dumbfounded. And proud — his daughter would earn more than he did.

Roessler found living quarters with the widow of the cathedral organist. Through the interest of a prominent woman in Graz, she had a letter introducing her to the Queen of Saxony; the latter took the young girl under her wing. The operatic roles she received were small, but she also sang in the cathedral. She was still weak at sight reading. On one occasion, with the king and queen present at the mass, she sang so badly that she infuriated the conductor. This finally convinced her that sight reading was important. A new conductor had her sing at Vespers for four years. She was given in turn the soprano, alto, tenor and bass parts to read at sight. At long last, she mastered sight reading.

When Roessler went home on vacation at the end of the first year in Dresden, she had two suitors. She refused them, but their proposals helped her self-image. She knew she was homely, but she had been paying more attention to her appearance. She also was working hard at self-improvement through reading.

At 18 she married Ernst Heink, secretary to the Royal Opera in

Dresden. They were both dismissed for having failed to obtain required permission. After some time, Heink found a minor position in the Customs House. He had debts that were difficult to meet. Soon a child, August, was born.

Through a music critic, Ernestine obtained small parts in the Hamburg opera. Her husband was transferred to the Customs House there. Then a baby girl arrived, foreshadowing Ernestine's fertility. With Ernst transferred to Saxony, three children now and only small parts assigned to her, she was discouraged.

But she was about to be surprised. A festival at which the Brahms Rhapsody would be sung was scheduled for Hamburg. The composer himself was invited and the conductor would be the renowned Hans von Bulow. Roessler-Heink was delighted to be assigned a solo. It was a tremendous success, and for the rest of her life, she remembered the excitement of bowing to the audience with von Bulow on one side of her and Johannes Brahms on the other.

Von Bulow gave her a big part in his forthcoming Mozart Cycle. However, when he learned that she was pregnant, he cancelled the offer. She did sing a few hours before delivery and was back at work in a few days. She was the family's chief bread winner.

Times were bad for her family. She had no money. The sheriff came to collect. She once became so desperate that she contemplated casting the children and herself in front of a moving train. She was actually about to do this, when she was deterred by her little daughter crying out that she loved her mama and wanted to go home.

A good neighbor named Frau Merton lived in the flat next door. A mother of nine herself, she tried to watch out for the Heink children when their mother was absent.

Despite all this, Roessler-Heink still had high professional hopes: she intended to be the first contralto not only in Germany but the world.

When it became clear that Ernst had deserted his wife and family, a tenor suggested that Ernestine might find work in the Kroll Theater in Berlin. With the train fare borrowed from Frau Merton, she arrived in Berlin at 5 a.m. and sat on a park bench until the theater opened. She was hired for summer performances, possible for her because she was not needed by the Hamburg Opera for that season.

As it became increasingly difficult to care for the children, she sent them to her mother. Later in life, she said her children and her art had equal priorities in her life. When her children were gone, she missed them very much; at the same time, moving up in her career became less complicated. Underlying her decisions was the essential fact that she had to support these children.

A great opportunity came when the conductor quarreled with the prima donna singing the title role in *Carmen*. Roessler-Heink knew the part and was able to perform without rehearsal. Colleagues lent her various items such as beads, a comb, a shawl and so on to create a credible character. She did well enough that next time the same star cancelled, the conductor used her as Fides in *Le Prophète* by Meyerbeer. A third cancellation by the temperamental woman gave Roessler-Heink a chance to play Ortrud in *Lohengrin*—again without rehearsal.

A new 10-year contract was made and this time she was paid a good salary; she would be given big roles and there would be important variations in the types of roles. She was still allowed to perform at Kroll and other theaters. Director Pollini also arranged summer concert tours all over Europe. At 27, Roessler-Heink was beginning to realize her aspirations. At this point, she borrowed money for appropriate costumes for her roles. She also started to use safety pins; until now she had felt she could afford only plain pins.

She had obtained a divorce from Ernst Heink. Through her theater contacts she met Paul Schumann, actor and stage manager. She married him in 1893 and henceforth was known as Ernestine Schumann-Heink. Paul had a child by his first wife, who had died. The four Heink children plus Schumann's son now formed a new family. Sometimes when Ernestine could not be at home, Paul would stay with the children and keep them informed about the details of her performance.

Although inclined to be jealous of his wife, he proved a good husband. His great knowledge of the theater was helpful to his wife in many ways. He offered constructive criticism; he gave her insight into the interpretation of the *lieder*, or songs, that became so popular in her repertoire. He had judgment.

When offered the role of the witch in Humperdinck's *Hansel and Gretel*, Schumann-Heink viewed it with disdain. Paul, though, saw its possibilities and convinced his wife that she would do well in it. It became one of her favorite roles.

There was a family story about *Hansel and Gretel*. One Christmas when it was being given, Ernestine let her children attend. They sat in a box, high up. When one of the little boys saw the witch pushed into the oven, he screamed that they were throwing his mother into the oven and were burning her up. He began to cry. Everybody looked up to see where the voice was coming from; Ernestine was wondering what would happen next. A few seconds later, she came out on the other side, to hear her son yell excitedly that there was his mother — they didn't burn her up.

There was a crisis when Ernestine's and Paul's first child arrived. The contralto was invited to sing in Leipzig when the baby was only 10 days old. Over her husband's objection, she went there, leaving a bottle because she could not nurse him. At the opera, her swollen breasts pained her. A woman in the chorus was having trouble nursing her baby, so for four days, Schumann-Heink played wet nurse to that emaciated baby.

Other stars tried to entice Schumann-Heink to America. She was interested, but did not wish to risk breaking her contract with Pollini. When the latter died, Maurice Grau, director of the Metropolitan Opera, sought a contract from her. It was arranged that the children would remain in Germany, with Paul's mother taking care of them. Ernestine pledged some of her salary as payment to Paul for stage direction or some similar activity.

There was one complication: she was pregnant again. Grau was perplexed, but there was little he could do. In November 1898, Schumann-Heink made her U.S. debut in Chicago as Ortrud in *Lohengrin*. The public went wild. Grau decided that her appearance in New York must follow the baby's arrival. That baby was named George Washington Schumann to show his parents' appreciation of their adopted country.

Schumann-Heink loved the United States and what it represented. She was especially thankful that there was no conscription. She had great admiration for President Theodore Roosevelt, whom she had met. She did not, however, approve of women becoming involved in politics.

In the summer season, she sang at the Covent Garden in London. In 1900, upon receiving a telegram stating that son George was dying, she walked out on the performance, thereafter losing her London audience. She returned to Germany, took over, and somehow the child survived.

Later she appeared at Wagner's Bayreuth in Bavaria. It was under the direction of Cosmina Wagner, the daughter of Franz Liszt. Schumann-Heink had been there before and always looked forward to learning from Wagner. She sang at Bayreuth regularly until 1903.

Grau resigned from the Metropolitan Opera in 1903 because of ill health. Schumann-Heink left too because she did not want to work under another director. By this time, some regarded her as the leading

Ernestine Schumann-Heink

Courtesy Library of Congress.

contralto in the world. Her repertoire included about 150 roles; her greatest fame came from her Wagnerian parts.

Returning to Germany where Paul and the children were, she found he wanted her to stay. She wanted to go back to the United States, which she did. She took a part as a German washerwoman in a comic opera entitled *Love's Lottery*. It toured in 1904-05. During a performance in Boston, she received the news that Paul had died. (He had been a chronic invalid for some time.) His mother died a few months later, so some new provision was necessary.

A month later, Ernestine married her secretary, William Rapp, a man 12 years her junior. "I felt that I must have his protection, not only for myself, but for the children," she explained. She retained her former name, but acquired American citizenship. The newlyweds went back to Germany to collect her seven minor children and one stepchild. (Her oldest was over 21.) They finally settled in New Jersey. The marriage to Rapp ended in divorce in 1924.

After *Love's Lottery*, Schumann-Heink concentrated on concert performance, returning occasionally to the stage of grand opera. One memorable event was her appearance in Dresden in 1909 in the premiere of Richard Strauss' *Electra*.

Schumann-Heink was in Bayreuth when Germany went to war in the summer of 1914. She returned home from Rotterdam in a ship carrying 3,000 — double its capacity.

August Heink, Ernestine's firstborn, was a German citizen with a wife and children in Germany. An officer in the Hamburg-American Line, he decided to fight for the Fatherland. He died on a German submarine. Two of her sons enlisted in the U.S. Navy, the rest, including her stepson, in the U.S. Army. One was drafted, and another died of typhoid pneumonia in 1915.

Schumann-Heink entertained American "boys" with her singing during and after the war. She even learned the words to "The Star-Spangled Banner" so that she could sing it on patriotic occasions. She had a deep interest in disabled veterans. She once said she thought her voice had given more happiness to the soldiers, and given her more happiness in singing for them, than she ever got out of her greatest opera days. At Camp Kearney, California, 120,000 soldiers crowded to hear her; there were more at a Memorial Day sunrise service in Cleveland.

By 1926, Schumann-Heink had become a popular guest star on American radio, a medium that she loved. She did an annual Christmas Eve broadcast and many concerts. At the height of her career, her voice was characterized by its excessive range. Recordings made as early as 1903 exist, and authorities note that the high quality of her voice showed very little deterioration until she was in her late sixties. Whatever the quality, her singing remained popular until she died. She made three appearances in the soap opera, *The Goldbergs*. She was sometimes heard on special broadcasts such as that celebrating the opening of the eight-mile Cascade Tunnel for the railway, when she sang "Land of Hope and Glory."

Some of her favorites were "The Rosary," "The Lost Chord," "Stille Nacht" and "The Lord Is Mindful of His Own." Here is a sampling of some of her renditions: "Lead, Kindly Light," "Die Lorelei," "Nearer, My God, to Thee," "None but the Lonely Heart," "O Come, All Ye Faithful," "Old Folks at Home," "Onward, Christian Soldiers" and "There Is No Death."

Ernestine had remarkable acting talent which showed up in various settings. In the 1920s, she made three movie "shorts." They were concert films in which she sang. In 1930, she sang for a week in vaudeville and later toured with it. In 1935, she had the part of a singing teacher in a movie called *Here's to Romance*, in which she sang "Wiegenlied" by Brahms.

Late in December 1926, she gave a concert in Carnegie Hall to observe the 50th anniversary of her debut in Graz. Later she made a 20,000-mile farewell tour. In 1932, she made a farewell appearance at the Metropolitan Opera.

She died of leukemia in 1936 in Hollywood, California. She had wanted to end her life in harness. Her wish was granted: At the time of her death, she had a three-year contract with Metro-Goldwyn-Mayer.

Ernestine Schumann-Heink was a strong personality. What she lacked in looks was compensated for by her native talent and presence. Her personality was related to her own contention that she was a child of the people. Although she had met hardships, she had received much kindness from friends and also strangers; this may have been what was reflected in her manner. Her personal travail during the war was especially severe, yet it represented the dilemma of other German-American immigrants who could identify with her. In the 1930s, she spoke out against the Nazi regime and did not visit Hitler's Germany. She had courage and faith and, above all, perseverance, setting her sights and refusing to be deterred. She loved America. America, in turn, loved her: A 1931 poll taken by *Good Housekeeping* magazine rated her as one of America's twelve greatest living women.

Evangeline Cory Booth

Today the mission of the Salvation Army is to preach the gospel of Jesus Christ and to meet human needs in His name without discrimination. It serves almost 100 nations around the world. Thus the organization represents an intermix of religion and charitable works. During her 30-year tenure in the American Salvation Army, Evangeline Booth immeasurably strengthened the institution, at the same time gaining for it additional respect and approval.

Evangeline Cory Booth was the seventh of eight children born to William and Catherine (Mumford) Booth. She was born on December 25, 1865, in the Hackney district of London. Her mother named her Evangeline for Little Eva in *Uncle Tom's Cabin*. However, the registry of births listed her name as Evelyne. The Booth family called her Eva; it was Frances Willard of WCTU fame who suggested that the adult Eva be called Evangeline.

As a young man, William Booth had been an apprentice to a pawnbroker. Much more to his liking was his lay preaching and outdoor evangelism. Converted at 15, he belonged to the Wesleyan Methodists. Conversion implied that an individual was born with original sin, but could be redeemed by accepting Christ as his or her personal savior. William entered the ministry of the Methodist New Connexion Church in 1852. By 1861, he had begun independent evangelistic work. Three years later — the year of Evangeline's birth — he and Catherine started in Whitechapel the East London Revival Society, which William named Salvation Army in 1878. Conditions in Whitechapel were unspeakable. Thousands lived in squalor with cholera rampant; smallpox was another threat. Unemployment was very high. Removal of a tax on beer had encouraged its increased consumption, so that alcohol was one of the major problems. (William once said, "The poor have nothing but the public house.") Worst of all, the people had no hope.

William seemed to understand their plight; he offered them the hope of the Gospel. The first services were held in a large tent erected in the Quaker Burial Ground. Enough people came forward as converts to convince William that he had found his life's work. At the same time, a philanthropist was sufficiently impressed to offer support of the endeavor. This foreshadowed the Salvation Army's course; the organization with the prime purpose of saving the souls of the destitute had sufficient appeal to make also possible material improvements. Thieves, prostitutes and drunkards were among William Booth's first converts.

Catherine was intensely interested in religion. She contributed ideas that were adopted. For example, she believed that women should be permitted to preach — so she preached, setting a precedent for other women Salvationists. She and William made a perfect team to carry on the work they both believed in.

One of the tenets of the organization was that after conversion, continuance in a state of salvation depended upon continued obedient faith in Christ. Baptism and holy communion were not considered important — this was Catherine's belief. Otherwise the doctrines were common to most Protestant evangelical denominations. The Salvation Army emphasized joyous singing, instrumental music, clapping, free prayer, personal testifying and open invitation to repentance. It also assumed a military atmosphere; the basic unit was the corps, commanded by officers named after military ranks — lieutenant and so on; Booth was General Booth. The uniforms had a military look, except for the black straw bonnets worn by the women; these were designed by Catherine. The motto was Blood and Fire — the former for the redemption that flowed from Christ on the cross, the latter for the spirit of the flaming love that glowed in the hearts of His followers. Gradually a program of social welfare was developed.

Evangeline grew with the Salvation Army, absorbing all the changes that it underwent. At an early age she was delivering sermons at home. Her pet monkey wore a miniature Salvation Army uniform until Catherine remonstrated: a man can change, but "once a monkey, always a monkey." Educated at home, Evangeline was well served throughout her life by that education. (The Booth children were educated at home after the oldest one was ridiculed at school because of his religion.)

According to her, Booth's childhood was very happy. She was devoted to her parents, and years later when some of her siblings deserted the Army, she remained fiercely loyal to the organization founded by her father. She believed that William Booth had divine guidance, and she therefore afforded him unquestioning obedience, similar to Francesca Cabrini's compliance with the decisions of the pope. In turn, Evangeline was a special favorite of William. She was converted before she reached her teens. Not yet an adult, she sang solo in a hall crowded with Salvationists. At 15 she became a sergeant in the Salvation Army. She was convinced that bringing souls to Christ was her mission.

Booth had been very successful at selling *The War Cry*, published by the Army. She read the issues before venturing out on the streets to sell. This enabled her to recommend specific articles, and the tactic often worked.

When she was 18, Booth was assigned to the Borough of Marylebone. Noticing that most of the children lacked toys, she collected sawdust from carpenters and discarded doll heads and limbs from a toy manufacturer to produce some for the deprived youth.

Surrounded by the poor, she realized she should know more about their situation. To understand the life of a young woman who was forced to earn a living on the street, she dressed in rags to sell flowers at Piccadilly Circus. She also sold matches at another location.

As a slum sister, she endeared herself to the people, becoming known as the Angel of the Slums. In addition, she learned to speak well at large meetings and to use her considerable musical talent. She brought about many conversions. Her work came to the attention of three members of Parliament who were known as humanitarians. They invited her to Westminster to question her about how a young woman like herself could have such a profound effect on hardened sinners.

The Salvation Army's activities were not always welcome, and there were many instances of persecution of these evangelists. Great opposition came from sellers of beer; in the year 1882, close to 700 Salvationists were knocked down or injured by these people. Booth, however, was never intimidated. She was happy to be bringing hope to the hopeless. It was in the London slums that she learned how the other half lives, an experience that deepened the compassion that exemplified her career.

With the title of field commissioner, she was given command of all Salvationist forces in London and the surrounding area. Her father also put her in charge of the Salvation Army's International Training College at Clapton. Clapton "cadets" received practical training and became familiar with official regulations, accounting methods and the like. A few could not read or write and had to be taught. The cadets were both male and female. Booth required that officers married officers or persons willing to become officers. His hope was that children of such unions would become officers, ensuring a supply of presumably reliable leaders.

Evangeline Booth served at Clapton for four years. One of her last orders was that each officer, prior to obtaining a commission, should be able to ride a bicycle. She had learned to ride and enjoyed the activity; it also solved some transport problems. A photograph taken at this period shows a very attractive woman with her bike. Her eyes were brown, her hair auburn and records note that she was 5 feet 10 inches tall and weighed 150 pounds. The athletic life she led gave her a good figure. According to some accounts, she wore a wig because a severe case of scarlet fever had affected her hair growth.

Catherine Booth died, or, to use the Salvationists' expression, was "promoted to glory" in 1890. She left her husband to live 22 lonely years without her. By that time, the Salvation Army had become international — the claim was that the law of God is international.

Towards the end of the 19th century, there were corps in many U.S. states. The National Commanders in the country were Ballington Booth, a son of the general, and Maud, Ballington's wife. These American commanders, however, took orders from London and were not in charge of an independent entity. In 1896, they left the Salvation Army and formed the Volunteers of America.

Evangeline took temporary command until Emma, her sister, and Emma's husband, Frederick St. George de Lautour Booth-Tucker, took over. Some credit Evangeline with holding the Salvation Army together when there was a possibility that its officers might defect to the Volunteers of America.

By June 1896, Evangeline was in Toronto as Canadian National Commander. The discovery of gold at Bonanza Creek in the Yukon brought hordes of people — good and bad — to that remote area. Booth made three trips to the Klondike, where Salvationists labored to rescue souls from sin. She also encouraged work among the Indians. Another of her enterprises was the Bureau for Missing Persons. Some schools in Newfoundland (not yet a Canadian province) were also started under her. Her tenure lasted for eight years.

Her next assignment was in the United States, where she would spend 30 years as national commander. She was 39 when she arrived in New York City. Since the American Salvation Army was 25 years old, some programs were flourishing and continued to grow.

Booth found in place a series of "working men's hotels" that provided adequate lodgings for low-paid urban workers and for some temporarily unemployed. The program grew, so that by 1908 there were 70 of these for men and for women, providing a total of some 8,700 beds.

One newspaper estimated that towards the end of 1908, 11 million people had heard Booth speak during the previous 12 months — a tremendous accomplishment in pre-radio days.

Comfortable and homey "rescue houses for fallen women" were proliferating. They were providing maternity services, and ultimately the Salvation Army would have hospital facilities to train nurses for this work.

There was increased emphasis on the ministry to children. An example of this was an all-day trip for 1,500 of Cleveland's poor children to an amusement park at Euclid Beach for lunch, movies and ice cream. It was financed by the returns from 11,000 mail appeal letters.

Growing also were "fresh air camps" such as the acreage at Camp Lake, Wisconsin, donated by the Chicago auxiliaries in 1904.

In 1906, a week's activity for the band of one of the Chicago corps included five open-air meetings, five indoor services, three musical programs for bandless neighboring corps and two practices. An extra obligation was a series of concerts to raise money for the victims of the San Francisco earthquake.

San Francisco was illuminated by kerosene and gas in 1906; fire broke out after the quake, and with water mains broken, there was little to check it. A large part of the city, including the Salvation Army's headquarters, was destroyed. In addition, relief work was handicapped by damage to some of its other installations: the Beulah rescue home in Oakland was wrecked, the orphanage in Lytton Springs was severely damaged and the Santa Rosa hall collapsed.

Oakland Salvationists opened their citadel and the Beulah Park camp meeting grounds to thousands of refugees. The military government detailed all willing Salvationists to help in refugee camps and emergency hospitals. The military also assumed some responsibility in maintaining Beulah camp; this freed up more Salvationists to work in San Francisco. Eventually most of the Salvationists from San Francisco arrived in Oakland, where that city's citadel was made the temporary headquarters for relief operations. The San Francisco workers had rescued hundreds of injured people placed for safekeeping in Mechanics Pavilion when it was realized that the building would burn. With a small fleet of industrial home wagons, the injured were transported to a ferry for Oakland, across the bay.

Booth staged a fundraising rally in New York at Union Square, collecting $12,000. Then she paid a visit to the scene of disaster, where operations were well under control. Almost 30,000 persons had been fed and more than 9,000 given beds; the Army was singing and testifying nightly at the refugee camp. At a mass meeting on May 30 in Golden Gate Park, she captivated the audience. Salvationists continued relief efforts throughout the summer.

When General Booth made his last official American tour that fall, he and his beloved Evangeline were received at the White House by President and Mrs. Theodore Roosevelt.

On Thanksgiving Day, 1909, a parade in New York City launched a great attack on Demon Rum. It featured a 10-foot papier-mâché whiskey bottle; there was an evangelical meeting addressed by notable saved drunkards from a New York City corps. This so-called "Boozers' Convention" became an annual event and was adopted by other cities.

Community centers in large cities were also developed to serve slum dwellers in various ways. This venture included family counseling because Booth was particularly concerned over the rising divorce rate.

By 1914, when war broke out in Europe, the prison ministry, previously so well managed by Maud Booth, was going well; a program to supply the poor with cheap ice in summer and cheap coal in winter had been expanded. More and more, projects such as these induced the public to contribute to the Salvation Army. Many non–Salvationists now associated the organization primarily with social reform, whereas early in the century, its work was almost completely centered on rescue. The official stance was that the Army's first responsibility was redemption. Booth believed that the first duty of a true Samaritan was to bind a man's wounds and heal his sorrows. Then the Samaritan must point him to God, who alone can make temporal assistance lasting.

In 1914, Booth organized a campaign to collect old but clean linen that could be processed for use as bandages and dressings in war-torn Europe.

The next year, second-hand clothing was collected for Belgian refugees. The German government occupying Belgium agreed to have a person from a neutral country manage the relief program. An American Salvation Army officer was chosen, and, financed from this country and London, served until America's entry into the war.

Although the Salvation Army prided itself in being international in its struggle against sin and strife, Booth offered her army of Salvationists for Red Cross work. Congress had authorized the American Red Cross to provide services for the sick and injured; the Young Men's Christian Association (YMCA) had authorization for social, recreational, educational and religious activities for able-bodied troops.

On the home front, the Salvation Army operated as one of the auxiliary welfare agencies under the YMCA. Before the conflict ended, 91 Salvation Army–run enlisted men's clubs were in existence.

It was the Salvation Army's presence in France that was remarkable. General John Pershing, in command of the American Expeditionary Forces, had a high regard for Salvationists. He permitted the Army to open its own huts and offer its ministry in the military district of the First Division. Booth borrowed a total of $125,000 to finance the Army's overseas work. (Money later poured in for this cause.) On August 12, 1917, seven men and four women — all officers — left to join Lt. Col. Willie S. Barker, whom she had sent ahead as the "pioneer to blaze the way for work in France." These workers wore regulation private's uniforms, marked with the Salvation Army shield on caps and epaulettes. Barker very soon requested more women. Single women officers in their twenties were sent to France. Only men not of gun-bearing age were chosen. The total number of Salvationists sent overseas did not exceed 500. Booth contended that they represented quality rather than quantity. Her brother, General Bramwell Booth, had succeeded William Booth as the international head of the Army, and he did not permit his sister to go to the front.

In Salvation Army huts, toilet articles, edibles and writing materials were available free or at a low cost. The Army offered credit to soldiers and provided ways to repay their debts with no red tape — a very popular service. The Salvation Army lassies — with orders to render selfless and cheerful assistance whenever needed — mothered the troops, commanding their respect. They darned socks, sewed on buttons, wrote letters, decorated graves; above all, they made doughnuts.

That started when Ensign Margaret Sheldon suggested that she and the girls with her bake something American for the boys in a camp of the First Ammunition Train of the First Division. One lassie wrote home about two women cooking in one day 2,500 doughnuts, 8 dozen cupcakes, 50 pies, 800 pancakes and 225 gallons of cocoa. Doughnuts could even be produced in large numbers by using melted lard in a bucket placed over a fire built below the surface. As troops moved from base camps to front lines, the Salvationists followed. Booth stressed that the enlisted men, rather than the officers, should be the focus of attention.

Commander Evangeline Cory Booth

Courtesy The Salvation Army National Archives and Research Center.

On September 12, 1917, the judge advocate general officially declared that the Salvation Army was a denomination of the Christian church. Its officers were thus exempt from the draft; however, on enlistment as chaplains in the military, they could receive commissions. General Pershing would say this regarding the Army: "Their one thought was the well-being of the soldiers. They came to serve." The overseas work of the Salvation Army ended the ridicule it had once endured; the organization was now commanding a new respect.

They were busy on the home front also. Booth established a War Service League in 1916, which eventually had a membership of 31,000. Members raised money, visited veterans in hospitals and knitted a vast number of articles for soldiers in the trenches.

The league also instituted a national drive for the prohibition of alcoholic beverages for the duration of the war. This would "kill two birds with one stone"—conserve grain and sugar, and, at the same time, reduce drunkenness. (Salvationists were jubilant when prohibition became the law of the land in January 1919, with the ratification of the 18th Amendment to the Constitution.)

Here is an excerpt from a speech made by Booth in 1922 at the opening of a training school for Army officers. This is how she regarded the contribution of the Salvation Army.

My father dreamed of a crusade extraordinary against the legions of iniquity—a crusade unconventional, unostentatious, unworldly, asking unprecedented sacrifices on the part of its followers in the interest of the immortal soul. From this one man's vision The Salvation Army sprang, its small and obscure beginnings giving little foreshadow of the mighty instrument of God it was destined to become, perpetuating the life-passion of its author among all people.

My father dreamed a troubled dream of the wrongs and wrecks submerged by modern civilization and mirrored in the glass of inspiration, he saw strong arms outstretched, lifeboats riding the wave and, a myriad salvage apparata at work for the rescue of human derelicts.

Thus were born the innumerable philanthropies of the Army's social wing, which has opened the vistas of possibility for the reformation, rehabilitation and regeneration of the pariah of society, and along which broken humanity has passes to newness of life, while outside this organization's immediate sphere it has blazed the trail for countless settlements of social welfare instituted by other denominations, for all which our hearts overflow with gratitude to God and afresh praise Him for our Founder.

Its war record established the Salvation Army as one of America's leading charitable institutions. By 1920, Booth had been its commander much longer than the customary five years allotted for a specific post. Bramwell Booth allowed his sister two more years, but prominent Americans wrote to London to protest her leaving at all. Bramwell yielded to this pressure. Clearly Americans liked her.

And she liked America. She became a citizen in 1923. She also bought a house in Hartsdale, New York. It accommodated her personal staff and had a stable for her horse. (She had taken up riding while still in England, under doctor's orders.) The grounds were beautiful; she planted additional trees and named them for relatives and dear friends. Her favorite was the Founder's Tree in honor of William Booth.

Some of her friends bought a property on Lake George and donated it to the Salvation Army for her use, with the stipulation that it could be sold later. An excellent swimmer and diver, Booth looked forward to spending July and August at this spot, which she named Camp Cory. Young officers from headquarters were often invited to Lake George for their vacations, and there were conferences there.

Booth possessed certain characteristics that made her a superb public speaker as well as a publicist. She had charisma; people felt her sincerity. She also had a flair for the dramatic — Vice President Thomas Marshall once noted that she could have been an actress (or a politician). She knew how to use flamboyant attire to accentuate a point; the same applied to her use of music. She looked impressive on horseback and sometimes rode in a procession. She spoke with ease to huge crowds.

She knew the value of music in the Army's mission. Late in her career she stated, "Sanctified musical talent is one of the most powerful means God has given man to help in bringing the world to His feet." Her favorite instrument was the harp, which she often played in public. She also both wrote the words and composed music for popular hymns, sometimes asking advice of professional musicians. Favorite hymns include "Fling Wide the Gates" and "The World for God." One of her earliest was especially loved. It was inspired by the sight of a 15-year-old mother with a dead baby in her arms. The desperate young woman was crying because there was no place for her to hide. Booth wrote, "The wounds of Christ are open ... There for refuge flee." It exemplified her great love for the poor and the young.

Booth's name was linked with several suitors. She never married although she said she would have made a good wife and mother. She raised four adopted children, one of which became a Salvation Army officer.

A competent administrator, she was skilled in choosing outstanding people to represent the Salvation Army and was always on the lookout for good officer material. She was a perfectionist, was sometimes impatient and was said to be vain about her appearance. For these reasons her staff sometimes found her difficult. However, they remained loyal to her, and her sense of humor could offset negatives. For her lecture entitled "The Shepherd," she ordered a white lamb. In Chicago her staff produced a poodle clipped to look like a lamb. Would she hold that instead? She agreed, but added that if there was one bark from that lamb, there would be trouble.

Although not a militant suffragette, she supported votes for women. She believed that woman's strongest influence was in the home. When conducting the marriage ceremony for one of her female officers, she used the word "obey," then said to the groom in an undertone, "Mind you don't ever tell her anything she doesn't want to do."

Booth's personality attracted various notables, who were often impressed by her. This of course was a tremendous plus for the Army's reputation and also brought in money. An example is her relationship with industrialist John Markle. She went to thank him for a gift of $10,000 to the Army. In the course of the conversation, she mentioned the need of a residence in New York where young business women could live comfortably at a reasonable cost. She came away with the $500,000 necessary to build such an edifice. Will Rogers, a less sophisticated type, contributed generously to her cause, while James Cardinal Gibbons endorsed her fund-raising.

In 1919, Booth launched the Home Service Fund. At the end of the first week, the banks in New York had a shortage of coins; the money had gone to the Salvation Army. This national campaign brought in almost $15 million, in the form of both small coins and large checks.

Booth recognized the importance of counsel from non–Salvationists interested in community affairs. Such people were made members of advisory boards and contributed much to the Army's progress.

A 17,000-mile tour of the states in 1922 convinced Booth of the effectiveness of prohibition. However, there was agitation to repeal the act — a movement fought by the Salvation Army. In fact, despite its nonpolitical nature, the Army, led by Booth, supported Herbert Hoover rather than Franklin Roosevelt for the presidency, since the latter was seeking repeal of the 18th Amendment.

Booth's ongoing concern was the succession of the general in command of the International Salvation Army. William Booth had set up a procedure whereby the presiding general would appoint his successor (as he had his son). Later, urged by Gladstone, William made a provision that if the incumbent were unfit — for one reason or another — a group of high Army officials comprising a High Council would be empowered to elect a successor. Some of the commanders, including Evangeline, found Bramwell Booth's leadership autocratic. They wanted him to retire and the opportunity to elect their own general.

With the Depression of the 1930s putting great strain on the Salvation Army's resources, Evangeline Booth arranged for a benefit football game between the Army and Navy teams. It was played on December 14, 1930, at Yankee Stadium, with gate receipts of more than $600,000.

Shelters for the homeless were provided by the Salvation Army in various cities: Chicago's was the largest, housing thousands. It was donated by William Wrigley, Jr., whose name was associated with chewing gum. The donated New York shelter accommodated more than 2,000 each night.

In 1931, another benefit was arranged by the National Broadcasting Company. Radio Land was held in Madison Square Garden and featured radio stars such as Bing Crosby and composers such as Jerome Kern, Irving Berlin and George Gershwin. The $500,000 raised from Radio Land was donated to the Salvation Army.

The economic situation became so critical that Booth requested her officers to take a 10 percent salary cut. She also closed for a year the country's four officers' training colleges.

Bramwell Booth rejected suggestions that he resign. Then he became seriously ill. The High Council met on January 9, 1929, and voted his retirement. An election on February 13 put General Edward J. Higgins in command. Evangeline had been in the running, but received only 17 votes to 42 for Higgins. She was disappointed, but knew that next time she would have a chance; the new system provided for election rather than appointment of a general. (Today 65 is the mandatory age for retirement officers.)

General Higgins retired in 1934. Booth was elected to succeed him as the Army's fourth general. She had to leave the United States, but would return when she retired. The affection and esteem of the people went with her.

In England, before Booth assumed her new duties at International headquarters, the American ambassador to the Court of St. James said in a public address, "England never gave a greater gift than when she gave us this good woman, this inspired leader. With admiration, respect and endless gratitude we give her back to you."

The position as general involved extensive traveling — to India, Australia, New Zealand and so on. In 1935, she attended a congress in Canada.

In 1934, she sent officers to begin Salvation Army ministrations in Singapore, Malaysia and Canton. Three years later, Army work was begun in the Philippines. In 1938, she had Salvationists working with refugees in Shanghai. The same year, she started an international youth movement.

Booth stepped down in 1939 when she was 73. She was succeeded by General George Carpenter. Back at her home in Hartsdale, she found retirement difficult. But her spirit was undiminished; she continued to ride Goldenrod, her horse, until he died and she herself was 81. She was "promoted to glory" in 1950 at the age of 84.

Evangeline Cory Booth, brought to the United States the gospel crusade of her British mother and father, reinforced by her own work on the London streets. Nepotism gave her opportunity; achievement was her own. The honors bestowed upon her — both here and abroad — are too numerous to note. When she received an honorary degree from Tufts College (now University), the president appropriately expressed her status:

> Not more by precept than by example you and those who labor with you translate into living purpose the great command, "Thou shalt love thy neighbor as thyself."

Senda Berenson

In 1892, James Naismith, the inventor of men's basketball, agreed to allow a group of girls to play the new game. The young ladies arrived at the gym clad in street shoes and wearing long trailing dresses with leg-of-mutton sleeves; several had what hinted of a bustle.

Within a year, Senda Berenson had girls in bloomers playing a modified version of the men's game. (Because of the bloomers, men were banished from the scene.) The adaptations of women's basketball by Berenson and her cohorts remained the essentials of the game in the United States for 70 years and brought enjoyment to countless young women.

Senda was the daughter of Jewish parents — Albert and Julia Valvrojenski (changed to Berenson). She was born on March 19, 1868, in Batremanz, near Vilma, Lithuania. In 1874, Albert emigrated to Boston. He was joined a year later by his wife and three children.

Albert became a traveling peddlar. He sold new pots and pans and collected used ones to be turned in to dealers. He worked hard, but had little money to spare for his growing family. At one point, Julia took in sewing and served meals in her home to earn money. Both father and mother had great expectations for their children, and they took advantage of the free education open to these children. It is therefore not surprising that an older brother of Senda, Bernard, after graduation from Harvard, became an authority on Italian art; he was also known internationally as a collector.

Once Albert saw Senda among a group of schoolgirls who had boarded his train. Afraid that she would be embarrassed to have it known that her father was a peddlar, he collected his wares and quickly disappeared from the scene by seeking another area in the train.

After elementary school, Senda began study at Boston Latin School (the girls and boys then studied at separate schools), but did not finish the year because of poor health. Later she studied piano at the Boston Conservatory of Music, but found it difficult to practice because of an aching back. By 1890, she was enrolled in the recently founded Boston Normal School of Gymnastics. She was there at her doctor's urging. At first she hated the curriculum. According to her, "Gymnastic work did not interest me and the simplest exercises made me ache all over." However, by perseverance she overcame her physical frailties and by the end of the first year was able to do all the required gymnastics. Such success filled her with enthusiasm for physical culture.

During her second year at the school, she "filled in" as a teacher of physical training at Smith College in Northampton, Massachusetts. The 15-year-old institution soon hired Berenson on a permanent basis, and she went on to have a distinguished career there.

Her first knowledge of Naismith's basketball came from reading a YMCA magazine. She considered the new sport "a quick spirited game" with one great fault — a tendency to roughness. On March 22, 1893, in Northampton, the Smith class of '95 played the class of '96, with Berenson as referee. Team members wore blue uniforms with distinguishing armbands — green for '95, lavender for '96. Each team had a song: '95's was sung to the tune of "Long, Long Ago," '96's to "Hold the Fort." The sophomores won 5–4, receiving from the defeated freshmen a white satin banner.

As the popularity of the game spread, there was little uniformity in the various sets of rules used by women's colleges. In 1899, the Conference of Physical Training, held in Springfield, Massachusetts, appointed a committee to address this. Its members were instructed to draw up rules that would incorporate as much as possible the various modifications that had evolved in different parts of the country. The committee consisted of Alice Foster, Oberlin College; Ethel Perrin, Boston Normal School of Gymnastics; Elizabeth Wright, Radcliffe College; and Berenson of Smith College. Berenson would edit official issues of the rules from 1905 until 1917. During the same period, she would also chair the Basketball Committee for Women.

To adapt the rules to women, the chief modifications were:

1. The division of the court into three equal parts to lessen the tax on the individual players when on a large floor.
2. The elimination of "star playing."
3. The encouragement of combination plays.
4. The removal of undue physical exertion.

Senda Berenson

Photograph by Epler and Arnold, Saratoga, New York, c. 1986. Courtesy College Archives, Smith College.

Snatching and batting the ball were eliminated. Holding the ball longer than three seconds constituted a foul. Only three consecutive bounces were allowed. Teams consisted of no less than six nor more than nine players each. Supervision by women coaches was strongly advocated.

The division of the court into three parts was a misunderstanding. Clara Baer of Newcomb College in New Orleans saw a diagram published in 1893 in which two dotted lines across the court were intended to show the relative spacing of players. When she interpreted these as restraining lines, the concept was retained because it was widely believed that the men's game was too strenuous and rough for women. Standards were set with regard to the size of the court, the number of players, the size and shape of the ball and the type of net. Various changes in the rules were made over the years, the major one being the division of the court into two halves with six players on each side. By the late 1970s, no differences existed between men's and women's basketball; five women on a team could move freely over the court.

Although standardization of the rules facilitated intercollegiate competition, Berenson did not approve of this type of competition. With the backing of the president of Smith College, she established there the precedent of non-participation in athletic events with other colleges.

Believing that "we should encourage the instinct of *play*, not competition," Berenson developed a strong interclass competitive program at Smith. Such an intramural program was intended to offer opportunities for all girls to participate, regardless of their level of ability.

Berenson considered basketball a complete educational experience; it offered exercise; there was intellectual, mental and emotional development through rules and decision-making, through self-control and through teamwork and cooperation. New students were encouraged to suggest new or better methods. Team captains served as coaches for their teammates.

Restrained behavior was required at interclass games. Sometimes gentlemen were excluded. The audience had to "limit the experience of their class enthusiasm to singing, and the penalty for shouting during the contest was the discontinuance of the game." A social activity followed each game. One such activity was known as a gym banquet, to which each member of the winning team escorted her particular rival and was responsible for seeing that the rival enjoyed herself.

Competition other than intramural was frowned upon by others besides Berenson. In 1923, led by Lou Hoover, then vice president of the National Amateur Athletic Federation and later First Lady, women prominent in physical education, recreation and the like met in Washington, D.C., for a conference. One of their resolutions stated: "Whereas, we believe that the participation of American women and girls in these [basketball] competitions was inopportune."

Writing in 1928, Ethel Perrin of the American Child Health Association noted that competition popularized basketball with boys and girls. She went on to say that this force proved to be a boomerang when used to excess. According to her, the development of super basketball teams of girls led to the inevitable result that winning the game loomed much larger in the minds of the backers of the teams, including the coaches, than the welfare of the participants.

It is clear, also, that women hygienists believed that very strenuous exercise was injurious to adolescent girls.

All told, older women involved in the supervision of female athletes seemed desirous of protecting young women and girls from the perceived evils that competition had brought to young men. These women decried publicity and admission fees to watch games. They even worried about how the girls dressed: Frymir, in her 1928 book, noted that it was unnecessary to sacrifice modesty in the costume for the sake of weight and comfort, cautioning that very short trunks or bloomers which are pulled up high on the thigh should not be worn.

Berenson had other professional concerns besides basketball. Her aim was to make the Department of Physical Training at Smith "as important in the life of the college as the academic departments." This was not a simple task; as late as 1901, she wrote, "a large number of people have yet to acquire the habit of exercising, have yet to learn that it is as necessary a part of the daily life as eating, sleeping, or walking." Berenson emphasized Swedish gymnastics in her teaching, and in 1897, became the first woman to study at the Royal Central Institute of Gymnastics in Stockholm. It was during a four-month course there that she learned advanced fencing. She introduced field hockey to Smith students in 1901.

Berenson was active in her community. She participated in home-culture clubs; she introduced Swedish gymnastics to Northampton High School and at Northampton Lunatic Hospital.

Loved and respected by students and faculty, Berenson remained at Smith until 1911, the year she married Herbert Abbott, a professor of English who became head of the department. For the next ten years, she headed the department of physical education at Mary A. Burnham School. The Abbott home was a popular place for Smith alumnae, faculty and students to visit. Mr. Abbott died in 1929 at the age of 64.

Berenson lived until she was 85. By 1922, she had crossed the Atlantic some 11 times; she had studied art in France, Germany, Greece and Italy. For many years, she lived in Santa Barbara, California, where she died in 1954.

Berenson noted that basketball "came in the moment when we were all looking for a game for girls that would prove interesting, that would have the element of team play, and that would develop strength and endurance."

It did that — and more. In the beginning, it aided in women's liberation by requiring nonrestrictive clothing that was far more comfortable than that in vogue at the time.

Title IX of the Education Amendments of 1972 prohibits sex discrimination in any educational institution or activity receiving federal financial assistance. Title IX provides the principal cause of action against sex discrimination in competitive athletics in education; one interpretation noted "a reasonable expectation that intercollegiate competition in [a] sport will be available within the institution's normal competitive regions." This implies the value of intercollegiate competition in women's sports — just what Berenson and others sought to avoid. Modern feminists encourage competition in all fields, and welcome support from Title IX.

Senda Berenson, an immigrant, was associated with the development of a popular game that contributed now and then to the emancipation of American women.

Helena Rubinstein

Helena Rubinstein had the ability to market successfully products and services that people wanted; she also invested her profits wisely. She was one of the noted businesswomen of the twentieth century.

Born on December 25, 1870, in Kracow (then under Austrian rule because of a partition of Poland), Helena was the oldest of eight daughters born to Augusta Silberfeld and Horace Rubinstein. This Jewish family lived in comfortable circumstances; her collections of miniature dolls and furniture provided the basis for the adult Helena's remarkable collections. She was taught to knit, sew and embroider. According to her, she was loved but not spoiled.

After a gymnasium education, Helena went to medical school at Horace's insistence. Unhappy there, she withdrew. Her father refused to allow her to marry a medical student who sought her hand; he favored as a son-in-law a rich widower of 35. At 18, Helena was not interested in this prospective husband. She decided to leave Poland.

A brother of Horace had emigrated to Australia. Helena had corresponded with his daughter, her cousin, and now she tried to arrange a visit to them. The uncle agreed, and Helen left Kracow. In her trunk were pretty clothes she treasured and 12 pots of her mother's beauty cream.

Her destination was Coleraine, a small town in the southwestern area of Victoria. She sailed from Hamburg to Melbourne via the Suez Canal. The journey from Melbourne to Coleraine was made by coach.

Life in Coleraine was a surprise to Helena. The dressy clothes she loved were out of place. The strong sun and violent wind were hard on the complexion. The women admired Helena's skin, and she responded by giving away some of the face cream provided by her mother. Soon Mrs. Rubinstein was sending her daughter monthly replacements. The composition of the cream is not certain. It was said to be the creation of a Dr. Jacob Lykusky who once lived in Kracow. Whatever the contents, the demand for the face cream grew.

Rubinstein's autobiography does not go into details, but it appears that the relationship between her and her uncle soured. She was determined to leave his home, but she was in a strange country and had little command of its language. She decided that somehow the skin cream would solve her problem. She contacted a young English woman she had met on the ship. This woman was married and living in Melbourne. Rubinstein arranged a visit and, at the same time, to teach German to the two youngsters in the family.

Slowly a plan evolved in Rubinstein's mind. She found another woman she had met aboard ship and negotiated a loan for £250. With some of the money she ordered a large supply of the cream in bulk. Jars and labels for portions of this were bought in Melbourne. She hand-lettered them herself. More of the money was used to rent and furnish a large second-floor area in a building in the city. The area was divided into three small rooms and furnished attractively and inexpensively. Rubinstein claimed that the curtains were made from white full-skirted dresses she had brought from Kracow.

Most women who came to the salon bought the cream. Rubinstein taught them the correct massage movements for applying the cream. She also tried to concoct different varieties of cream to suit different complexions. A woman journalist came from Sydney to see Australia's first beauty salon, and her writing spurred additional interest. Soon orders — including mail orders — far exceeded the supply. The upshot was that Dr. Lykusky himself cooperated in creating cleansing creams, astringent lotions and a medicated soap. Rubinstein worked very hard, devoting a great deal of her time and energy to business. According to her, at the end of two years, her bank balance had changed from a debt of £250 to a credit of £12,000.

More room was needed, and she found a seven-room suite, this time on the third floor. She also secured the services of her sister Ceska, then 18. Assuming that she would soon open shops in other Australian cities, Helena also began to train a small staff of beauticians. Thus began two practices that became common in her business: placing relatives in key positions and acquiring larger premises. Many years later, Helena explained that she always lived over the shops until there was a need to expand; next she moved into apartments; then she bought the apartments; later she bought buildings; finally she built buildings. She noted that real estate was a good investment.

In her twenties, Rubinstein was diminutive — 4 feet, 10 inches tall. Photographs of her show a good-looking young woman with very dark hair. During this period of her life, because she was pressed for time, she began to comb her hair back and pin it into a chignon. Work had become a compulsion. With Ceska managing the business, Helena could have taken time to enjoy other facets of life. She did not — she enjoyed creating, and could already envision her business in the great cities of the world.

She decided that she would briefly return to Kracow to visit her parents before learning more about what she considered scientific skin care. For her, that city had lost its former magic. She did learn from medical men in Paris and Vienna about metabolism and diet, the latest in facial surgery and so on. It is to her credit that through demonstration and writing she did try to educate the public about skin and hair care and related matters.

After she returned to Australia, she met Edward Titus, an American newspaperman of Polish extraction. An intellectual, he had friends in the literary and artistic world. Rubinstein was intrigued with this man who had vision and ideas. But when he suggested marriage, she wanted to run. She knew that she was too involved in her business to commit herself to that, despite the fact that she was in love with him.

She made plans to set up a salon in London, then at the height of Edwardian splendor. She knew that the decision either to stay or leave Australia would not make her happy. In her autobiography she explained her dilemma: "The truth is that my heart has always been divided — between the people I have loved and the ambition that would not let me rest." Titus's response was that soon he would follow her to London.

In London Rubinstein searched for a salon location that would be suitable for the elite of British society. At the same time, she was free to take in the plays of the day, watching performances by such luminaries as Ellen Terry. She also saw Isadora Duncan dance. The search for quarters ended when she found for rent a Georgian townhouse of four floors and 26 rooms. It required extensive renovation, but proved very satisfactory.

Edward Titus appeared in London and continued his campaign to win Rubinstein. He took her to the ballet to watch Nijinsky and to the Cafe Royal where she saw Somerset Maugham and George Bernard Shaw. When Titus proposed again, she accepted him. In the business world, she was known as Helena Rubinstein until her death. After a

Helena Rubinstein

Courtesy Helena Rubinstein Foundation.

honeymoon in Nice, the newlyweds lived on the third floor of the London Rubinstein salon.

By 1908, Rubinstein was convinced that women would soon be applying makeup. Actresses were using it to advantage, even if other women were inclined to shun it. Margot Asquith, wife of Liberal Prime

Minister Henry Herbert Asquith, was an exception, and some women moved to follow her example. There were ladies who visited the salon but took pains to avoid identification. But they came. Rubinstein claimed that within a year of the opening, she had more than a thousand clients who made regular visits. The editorial pages of society magazines made mention of the salon, and Titus composed attractive advertisements.

Through Mrs. Asquith and others, Rubinstein met a variety of people, some socially prominent, some who were intellectuals. Some had artistic talent; one was a titled woman, who, like Rubinstein, had a deep interest in interior decorating. She and Titus accepted the invitations of such people and in turn entertained them. She had always been interested in clothes and now felt strongly that a striking, exciting wardrobe was a necessity in the beauty business. Her favorite dress designer was Frenchman Paul Poiret.

With a baby expected, the couple bought a 20-room house near Putney Heath. Three Victorian hothouses were attached and these they converted to extra sitting rooms, each decorated in a different style. (One had a real fountain in the center.) Known as Solna, it was the place where Rubinstein spent more time at home than in any of the edifices she would purchase in the future. Here Roy Titus was born in 1909. Three years later, Horace arrived.

Helena's sister Manka was imported to run the London business. Another sister, Pauline, was in charge of a salon that had been bought in Paris, along with a line of herbal preparations. Helena thought, however, that the business there needed greater promotion. A restlessness overcame her, and when Horace was about 2, the family moved to Paris. There Helena was successful in attracting Parisian society to her salon, which offered Swedish massage in addition to the usual services.

In England, through the sculptor Jacob Epstein, she had started a collection of African sculpture. In Paris, she began to collect paintings, concentrating at first on abstract art. This habit of collecting would extend to jewelry and opaline glass; Titus collected manuscripts.

The family's next move was to New York early in 1915. Titus was an American citizen, and perhaps New York was more attractive than Paris during World War I. Whatever the reason for the relocation, Rubinstein viewed the United States as a huge market for her products.

With her husband and children completely settled in a house she purchased in Greenwich, Connecticut, Rubinstein set up her first American salon in a brownstone on West 49th Street in New York. Again, the ambiance was sumptuous, and journalists wrote about the amazing decor. She advertised her products, which were the bedrock of her business, and tried to explain any scientific basis for their use.

She moved Manka from London to work with her. By 1917, Rubinstein salons existed in San Francisco, Boston and Philadelphia — and soon afterwards in Washington, Chicago and Toronto. When doughboys returned from Europe with a new concept of emancipated women, gone was any aversion to lipstick or rouge. She was quick to take advantage of the situation.

The salons created demand by department stores to sell Rubinstein preparations. Helena accepted only large orders from well-known stores. Then she and Manka would train salesgirls in introducing, promoting and selling the products. They also gave private consultation to customers. Of course this involved much time spent away from home and family. The sisters wore Parisian clothes — one newspaper noted Mme. Rubinstein's "tomato-colored dress and eight strands of black pearls." (Twice a year, she regularly bought clothes from Paris designers.) This method of distribution of Helena's products was later carried on by her niece, Mala Rubinstein Silson. By that time, there were some 500 Rubinstein preparations.

After the war, Rubinstein and Titus returned to Paris. On the Left Bank, they built their own apartment house, complete with a private theater on the ground floor. Here some of Titus's protégés could have their works performed before a select audience. Rubinstein met Matisse and Chagall and other notable painters, sculptors and writers. Titus published a literary magazine and also books. He was on friendly terms with Joyce, Hemingway, Faulkner, D.H. Lawrence and e.e. cummings. Rubinstein was particularly intrigued by Mlle. Chanel, who introduced bobbed hair by cutting her own, who popularized short skirts, horn-rimmed spectacles, backless shoes and trousers for women, and of course, Chanel No. 5.

But all was not well in the Titus household. Edward was openly critical of his wife's frequent absences from home, and she made no effort to change her ways. Finally he told her that he had fallen in love with a younger woman.

When Lehman Brothers in New York offered Rubinstein $8 million for her American business, she sold it, with the idea that she could spend more time in Paris. It was too late; a divorce followed.

She then bought stock from Lehman Brothers until eventually she held one-third interest. The stock continued to decline in value after it left her hands, and when the stock market crash of 1929 caused an additional decrease, Rubinstein bought back her business with a net profit of $6 million.

Now middle-aged, she immersed herself more than ever in her work. Much of her time was spent in the United States, and she persuaded her sons to learn something about her enterprises. The business appealed more to Roy, the older one, than to Horace.

Copying the Bircher-Benner Sanitorium in Zürich, Rubinstein introduced some dietetic principles into the regimen of "A Day of Beauty." This proved successful except that the low-calorie lunch served lost money.

In 1935 in Paris, Rubinstein met Prince Artchil Gourielli-Tchkona, a Georgian 20 years her junior who would the following year become her second husband. She later described the 20 years of their life together as one of contentment and mutual esteem. The count died in 1956.

During World War II, Rubinstein was in the United States. Her London salon was bombed and her Paris properties occupied, but both businesses survived. In the early 1950s, the American business was grossing about $22 million annually. Gourielli was a New York subsidiary specializing in perfume. The Fifth Avenue offices employed several hundred people, as did the Long Island factory; there were salons in several large cities in the United States.

The personnel of Rubinstein's empire included Horace and Roy Titus, the latter serving as president of her board. The executive vice-president was Oscar Kolin, Rubinstein's nephew — and so on. Elizabeth Arden, archenemy of Rubinstein enterprises, referred to the family connections as a Polish mafia.

Rubinstein continued to run a network of houses, sometimes called Rubinstein Hiltons, in the United States and France. Her principal and favorite home was the penthouse apartment at 625 Park Avenue in New York. In all of them, she was continually rearranging the furniture, redecorating and adding "collectibles." All this she thoroughly enjoyed. After Gourielli-Tchkona's death, Rubinstein visited Israel, India, Thailand and Japan. In the latter country, she began negotiations that would eventually lead to the use of Rubinstein products by the Japanese.

She had little time for "good works." She did, however, extend a helping hand to aspiring artists. She also worked with the Maryknoll order of Catholic nuns to raise money and with the American Cancer Society. (She had suffered from cancer of the cervix.) She established the Helena Rubinstein Foundation in 1953. "My fortune comes from women and should benefit them and their children, to better their quality of life," she explained. The Foundation was a major beneficiary of her legacy when she died. Since 1954, it has disbursed and committed more than $76 million in grants. For 1994–95, close to $3.5 million went to education (48 percent), community services (25 percent), the arts (11 percent) and health (16 percent).

Twenty seven famous painters have done portraits of Rubinstein, including Salvador Dali. Graham Sutherland's portrait of her in old age was exhibited at Britain's Tate Gallery, with great acclaim. (Her hair was in what she termed the perennial chignon.) Picasso sketched her, but never completed the work.

Patrick O'Higgins, her assistant during the latter part of her life, wrote a biography entitled *Madame* that showed how well her mental faculties served her: She actively carried on her business until her death in New York at the age of 94.

Her autobiography was written just before her death. The second half is factual information on beauty — her legacy of expertise to women of all ages.

"Madame" attributed her success primarily to a combination of luck, hard work and perseverance. Obviously her vision played an important role. She also had a flair for public relations — for example, she launched "Heaven Sent," a fragrance, with hundreds of pale blue balloons floating down on Fifth Avenue; attached to each was a sample and the inscription, "A gift for you from Heaven! Helena Rubinstein's new 'Heaven Sent'." She was an artful adaptor: A Chartier lipstick case made for two lipsticks gave her the idea for her successful "Nite 'n' Day" lipstick.

Helena Rubinstein was sold to Colgate-Palmolive Company in 1973; in 1980, that company was bought by Albi Enterprises. After the mid–80s, the brand was discontinued in the United States. Cosmair, Inc., of New York hopes to launch the line at a future date.

Sophie Loeb

Sophie Irene Simon Loeb grew up in an era when a widowed mother in need had to turn to private charity for assistance in maintaining her family — Franklin Roosevelt's Social Security programs were to come. Loeb devoted her talents to improving this and related situations.

She was born July 4, 1876, in Rovno, Russia. Her parents, Samuel and Mary (Carey) Simon, were Jewish. When Sophie was six, her family emigrated to the United States, settling in McKeesport, Pennsylvania. The father was a jeweler. He died when Sophie was 16. Samuel left his family of three boys and three girls in straited circumstances. Sophie, who was the oldest, worked part-time in a store until she finished high school; Abraham, her 12-year-old brother, helped by selling newspapers.

After graduation from McKeesport High School, Sophie taught in that town's grade schools. (The requirements for teachers were less rigid than they are today.) Her earnings did much to make the family more comfortable.

In 1896, Sophie married Anselm Loeb. The owner of a store where she and a younger sister had worked, Anselm was much older than Sophie. Marriage changed the frugal life Sophie had lived. She gave up teaching and had time for music and art and poetry. She had a good voice and even produced a composition for the piano; she made designs to be painted on china; she began to write, and some of her essays on social conditions were published in newspapers, including the New York *Evening World*.

But Sophie was not happy. After a long period of indecision, she obtained a divorce in 1910. She moved to New York City, where she called herself Miss Loeb. She found employment at the *Evening World*, reporting and writing special articles. She was 32 and was described as small with brown hair and blue eyes.

Interested in social reform, she soon found a cause. It involved an issue with which she could readily identify because of her own family's circumstances — the plight of needy widows with young children.

In 1898, a "destitute mothers' bill" had passed both houses of the New York legislature only to be vetoed because of the opposition of state-supported orphanages and private agencies such as the Charity Organization Society of New York. This action may have reflected the attitude of some officials who were inclined to believe that recipients might not spend the money properly.

By 1910, President Theodore Roosevelt had convened a National Conference on Dependent Children that declared itself in accord with the concept of keeping destitute families intact. By 1913, 13 states had approved mothers pensions.

New York State did provide institutions for the children of poor widows. However, women who did not wish to send their children to such orphanages were dependent on private charity to keep family and home together. (As previously stated, there were private orphanages such as the one founded by Mother Cabrini.) It was clear to Loeb that private organizations could not raise adequate funds for this. Her aim was to have the state provide relief when this was necessary.

Most people believed that accepting charity was degrading. On the other hand, enlightened social workers of the day held that indigent mothers had the right to adequate assistance, and they emphasized the needs of the children. They tried to represent home relief, paid by the state, in this light, rather than to stigmatize it as welfare, which in reality it was. In line with this thinking, Loeb campaigned with the motto, "Not charity but a chance for every child."

Loeb found someone who had long worked towards her own goal — a social worker named Hannah Bachman Einstein. In 1909, Einstein had formed the Widowed Mothers' Fund Association to press the issue. Loeb now supported her with articles in the *Evening World*; she made speeches and tried to influence key people such as New York state legislators and the governor.

By 1913, both women were appointed to a state commission to study the problem. Early in 1914, before the outbreak of World War I, Loeb traveled on behalf of the commission to England, Scotland, France, Switzerland, Germany and Denmark — countries with advanced social programs — to learn about their provision of welfare.

Below are excerpts from the *Report of the New York State Commission for Widowed Mothers, 1914*. Approximately half is Loeb's report on her European study. Twenty-seven years later, authorities Schneider and Deutsch noted in their book that it reflected some very advanced concepts of contemporary social welfare.

Basic Principles

The commission believes it to be fundamentally true that:

1. The mother is the best guardian of her children.
2. Poverty is too big a problem for private philanthropy.
3. No woman, save in exceptional circumstances, can be both the homemaker and the breadwinner of her family.
4. Preventive work to be successful must concern itself with child and the home.
5. Normal family life is the foundation of the State, and its conservation an inherent duty of government.

The Situation in New York State

Two thousand seven hundred and sixteen children of 1493 widows are at present in institutions at public expense, who were committed for destitution only; 933 children of 498 widows are at present in institutions because of illness of the mother, resulting often from overwork and overworry that easily might have been prevented.

Public Prevention of Poverty

The problem of the prevention of poverty is perhaps the most serious that confronts any civilized community today. That it is ultimately preventable is a fundamental doctrine of democracy, an axiom of civilization. The principle of public effort in this field is an inherent part of the tradition of our State and Nation and is clearly recognized in our constitutions. The many laws which carry this great principle into effect must, from time to time, be modified and extended to keep pace with our increasing knowledge of the social needs of the community and our understanding of the methods of meeting such needs.

Alternatives Open to Widowed Mothers

The care given in the asylum may be more hygienic and scientific, but it is not, nor can it ever be, better than the care of the average mother.

The report included a proposed bill in support of destitute widows. Loeb was in Albany for the vote, but it lost narrowly.

Bitterly disappointed, she returned to New York City. She continued to fight, especially by using the press, and saw success the following year. The act provided for unpaid welfare boards throughout the state. Since lawmakers did not completely trust the bureaucracy, board members were granted authority to distribute public money to widowed mothers. It was stipulated that at least two members of each county board and three of each city board should be women.

Loeb soon became president of the New York City's welfare board, holding this unsalaried office until 1923. In an effort to keep the situation free of politics, she had trained social workers make investigations. She herself came to know many poor families. She became noted for her thrift, keeping the cost of administration at 3 percent. She was able to show that it cost the state less to maintain a child at home with the mother or a relative than to place the individual in a state institution, as required by law. During the first seven years of the board's existence, the city's annual appropriation was increased from $100,000 to more than $4.5 million. At the end of the period, the mothers of 30,000 children from New York City were subsidized in their homes.

As anticipated by the commission, laws needed to be modified and extended. Loeb worked to secure amendments to the original Child Welfare Act. In 1920, Governor Alfred E. Smith appointed her to a commission to codify the state laws in this area. Incidentally, the governor kept for her the pens with which he signed her various welfare bills.

Intending to encourage similar legislation in other states, Loeb wrote *Everyman's Child*, published in 1920. Part of it was serialized in *Ladies' Home Journal*. Four years later, she helped found the Child Welfare Committee of America. Her activities led to appearances before various state legislatures. Loeb was a speaker at the First International Congress on Child Welfare in 1925 at Geneva. That Congress adopted her resolution on behalf of "Home Life for Children as Against Institutions." Again in the international scene, the League of Nations in 1927 accepted her report on the care of blind children.

Loeb engaged herself in other reforms by publicizing and promoting them. Concerned about corruption in the New York Public Service Commission, in 1916 she prompted an investigation that resulted in the appointment of a new commission. She sponsored legislation that permitted the New York City schools to be used as civic centers for immigrants. She campaigned for cheap milk and penny school lunches, for making the movie theaters of New York City sanitary and fireproof, for cheap gas for the poor of Brooklyn, for lower taxi fares and bonding of drivers, for public baths, for play areas and for free maternity care for indigent women. She saw to it that movie theaters were kept

Sophie Irene Loeb
Courtesy Library of Congress.

open on Sundays. In 1917, as single mediator of a strike of taxi drivers, she settled the strike in seven hours. Late in life, she worked with philanthropist August Heckscher for slum clearance and housing reform. As radio became popular she used the airways as well as the printed page to advance her causes. People wondered where she found time to do so much volunteer work.

Loeb refused to run for public office and her services to the public were always given without recompense. Her newspaper work, speaking engagements and radio performances brought her about $10,000 a year. In 1913, she published the sophisticated *Epigrams of Eve* and three years later, *Century Fables of Everyday Folks* and *What Eve Said*. She had an apartment at Riverside Drive, a place in Miami and a summer home at Harmon-on-Hudson. At Harmon, she particularly enjoyed fishing.

In 1925, the *Evening World* gave Loeb an assignment in Palestine (now Israel) to write on the settlements. Her reports were republished in 1926 in *Palestine Awake: The Rebirth of a Nation*. Her experiences made her an ardent Zionist, and she donated the royalties to the Palestine fund.

Loeb died of cancer in 1929 at the age of 52. Ten years later, Congress amended the Social Security Act of 1935 with a provision for the protection of the widow and children of the worker in case of the latter's death.

Sophie Loeb, a childless woman, worked tirelessly for the benefit of children, earning herself the title of "godmother of American children." August Heckscher donated a memorial to her. Situated in Central Park, it was a round marble pillar encircled with carved characters from *Alice in Wonderland*; drinking fountains for children surrounded the base. Loeb herself had helped to establish the children's playground where the memorial was located. At the dedication in 1936, Mayor Fiorello La Guardia, the son of an Italian immigrant, praised immigrant Loeb as the "most unselfish woman I ever met who was active in public affairs."

Mary Pickford

Although she became famous and rich and her acting charmed countless viewers, Mary Pickford's life was a tragedy. Her existence was scarred by dependence on a domineering, although loving, mother; it was shaped by an adoring public that typecast her permanently as a sweet young girl; it was undermined by her own course.

She was born Gladys Louise Smith in Toronto on April 8, 1892. Her father, John Charles Smith, hailed from English Methodists. Her mother, Charlotte (Hennessey) Smith was of shanty Irish descent. Gladys was the oldest of three children. Their father held various jobs. In 1897, he sustained a head injury while working on a Great Lakes vessel; the next year he died as a result of that accident. He left his 24-year-old wife with Gladys, then almost 6, Lottie, then 2, and John Jr., a baby.

Charlotte Smith struggled to support her family through her sewing machine. She was soon approached by a stage manager who suggested that she could improve her financial situation by making actors of her children. Charlotte, in common with many others of her day, was opposed to the theater. However, a visit to the production the man had in mind changed her attitude. On September 19, seven months after her father's death, Gladys appeared for one week with the Cummings Stock Company at the Princess Theatre. She was paid $8 for playing two parts but speaking only one line at each of eight performances.

Later on, when another stock company — Valentine — presented the same play in Toronto, Charlotte persuaded the producer to give Gladys a part. In the spring of 1901, she again had parts with the Valentine Stock Company. In November, the show took to the road with 9-year-old Gladys a member of the cast. Two years later, all the Smiths had parts in *The Fatal Wedding*, one of the plays given by a D company on tour. (A, B and C touring companies were considered superior.)

The touring continued. Charlotte endeavored to keep her family together by obtaining some sort of a position for each of them in the same production, but sometimes had to entrust her children's care to adults she thought reliable. It was a hard life — the Smiths lived frugally, keeping a schedule that imposed many one-night stands. They traveled on trains and stayed in cheap hotels and boarding houses. Gladys obtained very little formal education. Her mother had been taught by nuns, and passed on much of her learning to her children. Gladys later claimed that she herself was a reader; perhaps that was the basis of her education.

A beautiful child with blond curls and hazel eyes, Gladys took to the theater, enjoying just about every aspect of it. Later in life when she was a stage personage with clout, she tried to create a pleasant work atmosphere similar to the one of her early experiences. Also, she was unusually intent on learning everything that would improve her acting.

By the time Gladys was 10, the Smiths were well acquainted with the Gishes — two daughters and their mother. The former, Lillian and Dorothy, would become noted screen actresses. Some summers when touring companies had little work, the two families lived together in a flat in Manhattan.

Because her salary supported her family, Gladys worked so much that she was deprived of an ordinary childhood. As an adolescent, she decided that if she were to continue in the theater, she would try to avoid road companies. If she could not get a job with a leading Broadway producer, she would quit the acting profession and become a dress designer.

When a play closed in 1907, Charlotte returned to Toronto. Gladys, however, remained in New York with a family she knew. Her idea was to be hired by producer David Belasco, a first step to the stardom she intended to attain.

Following an audition, Gladys was given a part in *The Warrens of Virginia*, at $25 per week. Her name was changed to Mary Pickford — taken from Elizabeth Denny Pickford, her paternal grandmother, and for Marie, the name Gladys preferred to Louise, the second name appearing on her birth certificate. The play tried out in Philadelphia then opened in New York in 1907. It remained on Broadway for one season, touring for a second. Through Belasco, Pickford learned the importance of heart, what he called "the capacity to feel." She would always be proud of her role as a Belasco actress. With regard to finances, at the end of the two years, she had $240 for her mother.

With the closing of *The Warrens*, Pickford found work with Biograph films in New York. She felt that the movies were beneath the dignity of a Belasco actress; on the other hand, the money that she would earn would keep the family together, avoiding their being sent to different stock companies.

In 1909, motion pictures were cheap entertainment. The audiences consisted of common people — shop girls, immigrants and the like. The usual charge to see a "flicker" that lasted from 30 to 60 minutes was a nickel. The show changed every day.

Pickford's first appearance with Biograph was in *Her First Biscuits*, directed by D.W. Griffith, who even today is remembered as the director of *The Birth of a Nation*. She would play various roles in more than 100 Biograph films. As with the theater, she was determined to learn everything important about filmmaking. By 18, she was a star.

She once wrote, "Of all the elements of character, I think self-analysis is the most important." Such analysis brought her security in giving expert portrayals of children, adolescents and girls/women. She believed that her stature and general appearance did not bode well for great emotional roles. At the beginning of her film career, she weighed 115 pounds, rather much for her height of five feet, one inch. Later on, she weighed about 95 pounds and measured 33¼–25–36. Her blond curls had become golden brown, but she was photogenic and imparted sweetness and innocence. Apparently this is what appealed to the public for many years. To exemplify — when she was 24 and earning more money than the president of the United States, to the public she was between 12 and 16. Her image was helped by the fact that she added fake curls to supplement her own. (They came from prostitutes and cost $50 each.)

In an effort to keep their salaries low, Biograph did not bill or publicize actors' names; fan mail was not delivered to the one for whom it was intended. This was one factor in Pickford's leaving the company in December 1910. (She returned briefly at a later date.) She was ambitious and intended to be known in her profession. The question of professional acclaim was bound up with salary, and Pickford was most aggressive in her demands for money and special concessions. As supporter of her family, this was necessary. Charlotte could drive a hard bargain and was often instrumental in the realization of Mary's demands. Reporter Adela Rogers St. Johns once noted that Charlotte's relationship to her daughter was that of a sculptress to her masterpiece.

There was another factor in Pickford's leaving — she had become

Mary Pickford

Courtesy Library of Congress.

interested in a man named Owen Moore. When he left Biograph to work for Independent Motion Picture Company, Pickford followed him. At the same time, through IMP, she became identifiable as the girl with the curls.

She married Moore in secret and did not tell Charlotte for some time. Perhaps Charlotte feared that marriage per se would hurt her daughter's image as an innocent young girl; certainly Charlotte did not regard Moore as a promising husband for her beloved daughter who was at the same time a good meal ticket for the family.

The marriage was shaky from the beginning. Charlotte's opposition did not cease. Pickford continued to make more money than Moore, at the same time becoming more and more famous. The situation may have contributed to his insecurity and constant drinking. A divorce became final in 1920.

After Griffith, Pickford made pictures under Adolph Zukor, who publicized her image as "America's Sweetheart." He did little to let it be known that she was a married woman. By 1915, she was receiving some 500 fan letters a day and dividing her time between New York and Los Angeles. That year Zukor's Famous Players and Jesse Lasky's Company combined to form Paramount Pictures. The chairman of the board was Sam Goldfish, later to be known as Goldwyn. The Lasky Company had Cecil B. DeMille's films, estimated to bring in great profit, and Zukor had Pickford, considered by Lasky "a property of inestimable value." Her fame was built on leading roles in such pictures as *Tess of the Storm Country*, *Pollyanna*, *Rebecca of Sunnybrook Farm* and *Poor Little Rich Girl*. Pickford considered herself worth more than Charlie Chaplin, whom she regarded as a mere comedian, and she did not fail to let Zukor know that she expected more.

The suffragist cause was not one of Pickford's interests. However, in 1917, her salary was $560,000, and her studio was netting close to a million dollars from her films. That would have seemingly advanced the feminist cause by convincing the public that earning a great amount of money was not the exclusive province of a man. Incidentally, she saved $420,000 of that salary for investment. She became very shrewd at real estate transactions — for instance, she once sold for $200,000 a piece of land she had bought for $3,000.

As Herndon pointed out in *Mary Pickford and Douglas Fairbanks*, "America's Sweetheart," the highest paid woman in the world, was really uneducated, shy and insecure. She was very close to her family, but had few friends except for Frances Marion, a screenwriter of whom she was fond. She did not really enjoy the money she was making; the poverty of her early days still haunted her, making her fearful of losing what she had. Most serious of all, she was involved in an unhappy marriage.

In 1917, a romance began between Pickford and flamboyant actor Douglas Fairbanks, who was ten years her senior. Both were married, so the outcome was in doubt. But Pickford certainly fell in love. That year, both were working in Los Angeles and often managed to meet in secret.

The third Liberty Loan drive brought them together legitimately. To sell bonds to help the war effort, Pickford, Fairbanks, Charlie Chaplin and William S. Hart went to Washington, D.C., on April 6, 1918 — the official opening day of the third Liberty Loan and the first anniversary of the country's declaration of war. They raised huge sums for the cause, and Pickford and Fairbanks were able to travel across the continent for five days on the same train and then spend time in the nation's capital and in New York. After that, Pickford continued the drive with a tour of the northwest. (She also bought thousands of dollars worth of Liberty Bonds and contributed generously to the Canadian War Loan.)

Meanwhile, Mrs. Fairbanks announced to the press that she and her husband were separating. They ultimately divorced.

When Fairbanks urged Pickford to marry him, Charlotte tried to prevent the union. He had little use for her family; in particular, as a teetotaler, he detected alcoholism in both Jack and Lottie. At the age of 12, he had promised his mother not to drink until he was 40, and he kept his word; his father had been an alcoholic who deserted his family. Fairbanks was not fond of Charlotte, but to keep peace, he avoided open quarrels with her. It is likely that he perceived the animosity she felt towards him. When he finally told Pickford that he would wait no longer, she defied her mother and tried to ignore her own fear that marriage to a prominent but divorced man with a child might destroy her public image. They — two divorced Catholics — were married on March 28, 1920, by a Baptist minister in Glendale, California. (Pickford later became seriously interested in the teachings of Mary Baker Eddy.)

Pickford's anxiety had been misplaced. On their honeymoon trip to New York and Europe, they were as popular as ever. This was unexpected, because in 1920, divorce was not condoned as it is today. There was one bar to Mary's happiness: She soon discovered that her husband was almost pathologically jealous — to the extent that he became infuriated if she danced with another man.

In 1919, Pickford and Fairbanks joined Charlie Chaplin and D.W. Griffith in forming United Artists to produce their own films and control the distribution of them. The company would, of course, have to find investors, for film production was very expensive. William Hart, noted for his roles in Westerns, had intended to be a founder, but backed away when it was time to put up the required $100,000. Pickford was not married to Fairbanks at the time, but together they bought a studio in West Hollywood. Colleagues and underlings remember them as considerate and kind.

In the first two and a half years of the existence of United Artists, Pickford made five films. One of these was *Little Lord Fauntleroy* in which she played a dual role — the boy and his mother. It was co-directed by Jack Pickford (Smith), her brother. Pickford was also involved in the company's operation, with her mother empowered to speak for her as a stockholder. The star was interested in the selection of films and sometimes chose to remake previously released titles. When it came to a choice between artistic and commercial interests, she bowed to the latter. By 1924, it was necessary to bring in additional talent in the form of Buster Keaton, Gloria Swanson, John Barrymore, producer Samuel Goldwyn and others, but the company prospered.

In 1919, Fairbanks purchased a hunting lodge in a remote mountainous area outside Los Angeles. Remodeled, it became known as Pickfair, the home of the king and queen of the cinema. (The population of Beverly Hills in 1920 was 672, but the rapidly expanding movie industry was converting Los Angeles to a populous center.) Pickfair had stables for riding horses, a swimming pool and ample room for guests. The visitors included royalty, millionaires and sports celebrities. Actors and actresses were still considered an immoral lot, but the Fairbankses and their visitors helped to improve Hollywood's image. Despite their own history, the movies' leading lights did not welcome couples having illicit affairs, and because of Fairbanks' feelings, little liquor was served.

He was more inclined to spend money than Pickford, exemplified by the fact that he gave her gifts such as an 182-carat sapphire called the Star of Bombay. He loved to travel, which could also prove expensive. In the fall of 1921, they spent almost a year abroad. Leasing a home in Paris, they promoted their films all over Western Europe. Charlotte and Lottie came along, as well as a retinue of valets, maids and secretaries with 43 trunks. Pickford enjoyed herself, but she definitely did not have her husband's wanderlust; she would have preferred to be home making pictures. This she loved, and it brought in money. By 1929, the Fairbankses had made seven trips to Europe. Before that, Pickford had noticed an increasing restlessness about Fairbanks.

Charlotte died in 1928 from breast cancer. Of her million dollar–plus estate, the bulk went to Mary, with Lottie and Jack receiving trust funds of $100,000 each. Pickford missed her mother's support very much, but her new-found independence was apparent when, three months after Charlotte's death, she cut her curls.

Her next deed was to take a talking role. Actors and actresses worried about how the quality of their voice would be received, how popular would an accent be and so on. In the silent films, facial expression was more important than when much could be expressed vocally. So no doubt Pickford was apprehensive. She chose the drama *Coquette*, in which she, at 35, played a college student. She must have done creditably, for her performance won the award (Oscar) of the Academy of Motion Picture Arts and Sciences for Best Actress (1928–29). Pickford had co-founded the academy two years earlier.

When she returned to Toronto in 1934, the police reported that more people came to see Mary Pickford than had paid tribute to the Prince of Wales who was slated to be crowned Edward VIII. Pickford could have technically been an American citizen by marriage, yet she traveled with a Canadian passport and took pride in being a Canadian. (However, the Order of Canada for distinguished citizens was denied her because she left the country at an early age and had returned infrequently.)

Fairbanks and Pickford combined their talents to make *The Taming of the Shrew*. Following that they sailed for Europe. They visited Egypt; they took a ship through the Suez Canal; they sailed on to India, Southeast Asia, China and Japan. When their ship docked in Los Angeles on January 3, 1930, Pickford had had enough of world travel. She had to be working — she would make films and attend to her business affairs; Fairbanks could go wherever adventure beckoned.

After 12 years, the Pickford-Fairbanks marriage was in trouble. He would take off on long travels without her, sending home numerous telegrams. There is some evidence that he found substitutes for her. She was finding solace in alcohol, although few people knew it. With her mother dead and her husband away, her loneliness was alleviated by an attractive young actor known as Charles Buddy Rogers.

Fairbanks realized his wife's liking for alcohol and her infidelity, yet he did little to spend more time with her. After he had been named correspondent in a divorce case in England, Pickford filed for divorce, which became final in January 1936. Friends believed the Fairbankses were still in love with one another, but each was selfish in his or her own way. According to her stepson Douglas Fairbanks, Jr., it was after the divorce that Pickford's drinking really stepped up.

Pickford's last movie was *Secrets* in 1933. It was not a financial success, and being a shrewd business woman, she saw the handwriting on the wall. It has been pointed out that the operative word of Hollywood was fear; Pickford's fear must have at least been of old age, talking pictures and increasing competition. (In contrast to her realism in business, she followed astrology and consulted mediums about contacting her mother and also Fairbanks after his death in 1939.)

The years 1910–25 include her great acting triumphs. She continued to direct until 1949. She remained active in United Artists until 1956, when she sold her interests for $3 million. She provided a fund of $250,000 to restore and preserve as many as possible of her films.

In 1934, Pickford tried her own radio show; it was short-lived. She had some talent for writing. Her 1934 ghostwritten *Why Not Try God?* was a bestseller. The following year, *My Rendezvous with Life* appeared, as did a novel entitled *The Demi-Widow. Sunshine and Shadow*, an autobiography, came out in 1955.

Buddy Rogers and Pickford were married in 1937. He was handsome and well-liked. Some 12 years her junior, he had met her ten years earlier. His acting career held no great possibilities, but he was a musician and had organized an orchestra that played in major cities. He and Pickford moved into Pickfair, which was hers. With her obviously the family boss, the marriage lasted for 42 years. Rogers did not have Fairbanks' marked aversion to alcohol, but he covered up her indiscretions.

Pickford yearned for children. According to Eyman's book, she had had an abortion when married to Owen Moore. Some believe that this had made her sterile. At any rate, when she was 51, Pickford and her husband adopted a 6-year-old boy. Two months later, they found him a 2-year-old sister. Pickford was also strongly attached to Gwynne, daughter of Lottie, who had died in 1932 of alcoholism. (Four years earlier, Jack had died of the same disease.)

In retirement, Pickford's alcoholism became more apparent to outsiders. At the premiere of *Sleep My Love* in Ottawa in 1948, she made a rambling speech but was cut off by someone in her party who realized her condition. A few years later, when an old friend took her to lunch, she got so inebriated that she fell forward into her food. In 1959, her old sound technician reported attending a board meeting at which Pickford was clearly in an alcoholic stupor.

On the positive side, Pickford worked hard for the Motion Picture Relief Fund and Home. In 1953, she went on a coast-to-coast tour with Mamie Eisenhower to sell savings bonds. She had other philanthropic interests such as the Orphans' Asylum, a Catholic institution, and the Jewish Home for elderly Jews, both in Los Angeles. In 1961, Middlebury College conferred on Pickford an honorary degree for "her lifelong dedication to causes and actions of benefit to her fellow men."

In 1965, she and Rogers were in Paris for a month-long tribute to her films from Cinémathèque Française. Having worked hard to learn to speak fluent French, she was proud of her ability to address the audience in its own language. Later she said that of all the honors she had received that tribute touched her the most.

By 1972, Pickford had become a recluse. According to biographer Robert Windeler, she did not wish people to see her as an old lady. An honorary Academy Award was bestowed on her in 1976. She did not appear in person to accept it, but the audience saw a film of the presentation of the gold statuette to a tiny, fragile old woman.

She died in 1979. After cremation, her ashes were interred in the Pickford family vault with the remains of Charlotte, Lottie and Jack.

In 1917, a well-known movie magazine held a popularity contest, and Pickford won almost twice the number of votes of her nearest competitor. After *Secrets*, she said, "I could have gone on and done more mature parts, but ... I think it was the public that wouldn't accept it." Her friend Lillian Gish was successful when she moved to more mature roles, but Pickford seems to have been correct in judging her fans' reaction about herself. She thought it best to let her reputation stand as it was.

And that reputation? In 1931, Benjamin Hampton, an industrial leader of the day, wrote: "Mary Pickford is the only member of her sex who ever became the focal point of an entire industry. Her position was unique; probably no woman, or man, will ever again win so extensive a following."

Dorothy
Jacobs Bellanca

Having worked in a clothing factory as a young girl, Dorothy Jacobs Bellanca was familiar with the deplorable conditions that were allowed to exist in industry early in this century. At 16 she decided to devote her life to organizing workers; she was convinced that union membership would bring them a better life.

Dorothy was the youngest of four daughters of Bernice Edith (Levinson) Jacobs and Harry Jacobs. She was born August 10, 1894, in Zemel, Latvia, to Jewish parents. Six years later, the family emigrated to Baltimore, where Harry worked as a tailor. Bernice died a few years later. Dorothy attended public schools in Baltimore until she was 13.

At that age she took a job that required hand-sewing buttonholes on men's coats. After spending four weeks as an unpaid apprentice, she was able to earn $3 a week. The working day lasted 10 hours; when her fingers became infected, forcing her to stop work temporarily, her pay stopped also.

It was not unusual for a 13-year-old to be doing such work. Jewish parents — and there were many Jews in the garment industry — took comfort in the fact that their children were among others of their ethnic group and therefore under some protection.

Jacobs began to press co-workers to join a union. Her employer warned her that she must stop, but his order fell on deaf ears. By 1909, she had organized Baltimore immigrant women buttonhole makers into Local 170 of the United Garment Workers of America (UGWA). This union was organized on traditional craft lines; the majority of the members were American-born conservative workers rather than immigrants.

In 1910, clothing workers in Chicago were on strike. Fellow clothing workers in Baltimore were asked to donate clothes for them. Jacobs recalled that this alerted her to the power of collective effort and motivated her to become an activist.

By 1910, trade unions had made some progress, but radical reforms were needed. The average wage for industrial employees was 28 cents per hour, with the average work week being less than 55 hours. The increase in immigrants kept pay scales low because these newcomers were inclined to work for less than workers born in this country. Women received less than half as much as men. Faced with low pay and poor working conditions, more and more industrial workers joined unions.

The public was not receptive to organized labor; farmers in particular were opposed. People were generally afraid of strikes and tended to back the business community. They believed that radicals ran the labor movement and would undermine the nation's economic and political stability. In that era that prized individual accomplishment, there was a feeling that a man without a job was that way because of his own deficiencies.

By the time she was 20, Jacobs was organizing machine buttonhole makers, most of whom were men — many of them immigrants. She and some other women visited the homes of prospective members. According to Jacobs, if some of the men were unreceptive, "we would appeal to their wives, or any members of their families who were open to argument or conviction."

In 1914, Henry Sonneborn and Company of Baltimore planned to modernize their machinery and then renew production with fewer workers at lower pay. The employees discovered this plan. On October 1–3, 3,000 garment workers from the company went on strike. Some belonged to the UGWA, but most were not union members. They were joined by other clothing workers.

The strike clearly demonstrated two factions in the UGWA. The first was composed of older and more skilled workers such as cutters who were for the most part native-born. The second faction was composed of younger, less skilled immigrant workers, represented by machine operators. The UGWA's Sidney Hillman, a Lithuanian immigrant and former skilled cutter, advocated industrial unionism, whereby workers — skilled or otherwise — joined the same trade union to unite against the abuses of industrial capitalism.

The Baltimore strike established Jacobs as a woman labor leader. She addressed many meetings of strikers and also served on the picket line for the duration of the 13-week strike. The workers came to refer to her as "Our Dorothy." A settlement was finally negotiated by Hillman.

In December 1914, a new union named the Amalgamated Clothing Workers of America (ACWA) was founded at a meeting in New York City. It was composed mainly of the young, less skilled immigrant workers of the clothing industry. Older and more skilled workers remained in the UGWA. Amalgamated included Jacobs' Local 170. She was one of 175 delegates, five of whom were women. Sidney Hillman was elected the first president. Sonneborn's agreement granted union recognition to almost 3,000 new ACWA members.

The second biennial convention of the new union was held in Rochester, New York, in 1916, and Jacobs again represented Local 170. Later that year, she became a member of the union's seven-person General Executive Board; not yet 22, she was an officer of her union. The following year, she was appointed its first full-time women's organizer.

In 1918, Jacobs married August Bellanca, an ACWA organizer and member of the General Executive Board. Born in Sicily, he had emigrated to the United States when he was a young man. Despite religious differences and the many separations that their work imposed, the couple had a happy marriage. They had no children. Both served ACWA with great constancy. (Another husband and wife team of organizers was the Hillmans — Bessie Abramowitz had married Sidney Hillman in 1916.)

Between 1914 and 1920, American unions showed an average growth of 90 percent. The ACWA's growth had nearly tripled that rate. In the post-war years, when there were fewer government contracts, union membership declined. There were other reasons: Employers were inclined to move businesses to non-unionized areas where cheap and seasonal labor was available; in addition, a few employers were offering job security and fringe benefits such as medical services.

Dorothy resigned from the General Executive Board when she married August. Her advice was often sought by her successor, Mamie Santora. Both were women leaders in ACWA's Out-of-Town Organization Committee. Bellanca's chief concern became the organization of women in the so-called "runaway" shops in non-unionized areas throughout New York, New Jersey, Pennsylvania and Connecticut. She encouraged their worker to join ACWA. She also spoke out against the paternalism of the new welfare capitalism of employers, stressing that what the boss gave, he could take away. Her aim always was to educate women (and men) about the benefits of collective bargaining. In January 1921, she concluded an address to Local 170 with an appeal for 25 cents a week from each member to be given to a milk fund for babies affected by a lockout in New York City. She got the money despite the fact that these members were already docked for 10 percent of their wages, the money earmarked for the New York lockout fund.

August Bellanca became ill in the spring of 1922. So that he would be free of union worries, he and his wife sailed in the *Majestic* to his native Italy for a long rest. Thus Dorothy took a leave of absence from May 1922 to May 1923. (Some 30 years later, ACWA members paid for the Dorothy J. Bellanca Auditorium in the Boys' Republic at Santa Marinella, a village near Rome for homeless boys.)

Bellanca was convinced that women were a permanent part of the work force; she continued to fight for conditions that particularly concerned them. With this in mind, she pressed for a separate Women's Department, envisioning "a closer relationship between our women members and the organization." In July 1924, ACWA invited her to direct such a just-established department. She agreed to serve, but without compensation. She hoped that the actions of the Women's Department would convince the male members of the union that women played a significant role in trade unions — not all the men in ACWA were as receptive to women organizers as August Bellanca.

The Women's Department was not a success; some of the male members resented the separate attention that was being provided in the form of social functions, private meetings and so on, to new female recruits. In order to end any activity that threatened to divide the organization, Bellanca proposed in 1925 to dissolve the department. Hillman and Mamie Santora agreed with Bellanca's thinking that harmony in the union was paramount.

By 1928, the ACWA membership was only 700, down from 3,000 eight years earlier. Gains in membership had been made in New York and Baltimore, but close-by Philadelphia was known as "the graveyard of unionism." Three years earlier, a plan to organize that city had failed. The current plan was for ACWA to conduct a shop-by-shop campaign. August Bellanca's task was to organize Italian workers, to whom he often spoke in Italian; Mamie Santora organized female Italian workers; Dorothy Bellanca worked with Yiddish women, and so forth. According to Dorothy, it was hard work — "this going to people who had their minds poisoned against the organization, and trying to convince them that the union is a good thing."

But there was victory: By October 1929, 92 percent of Philadelphia's clothing workers — more than 10,000 people — had joined ACWA. At the celebration that followed, the letters "ACWA" were formed by members on the dance floor. The Bellancas were present at the festivities.

Dorothy Jacobs Bellanca

Courtesy Labor-Management Documentation Center, Cornell University.

In 1932, ACWA called a general strike to alert the public to poor pay scales and shameful working conditions that now existed in Baltimore. When Bellanca spoke at a meeting, "her ringing voice and the emotion and feeling which she shared made everyone feel her compelling sincerity." She and Mamie led a group to the office of Mayor Howard W. Jackson to request help.

After five months, ACWA declared success. The mayor had commissioned economist Jack H. Hollander of Johns Hopkins University to investigate working conditions in the garment industry. A report by the commission he set up made people realize the abuses and also that the police had evoked an outmoded law to arrest 150 women who had been picketing peacefully.

Bellanca's union had not only grown, it was progressive. Hillman realized that union businesses must be competitive, and he was a leading exponent of scientific management. The ACWA cooperated with manufacturers to make better products at a lower cost, to produce new lines and, if necessary to preserve jobs, to extend credit to owners.

In Chicago and New York, the union opened labor banks that survived the Depression. These banks paid high interest rates to small accounts and loaned small sums to workers who could not borrow from commercial banks. They even saved some employers from bankruptcy. The ACWA banks also financed a low-cost housing project in New York City; the union members paid roughly a third of the amount paid by non-ACWA persons for comparable accommodations.

As the Depression deepened, Hillman called for a large-scale national recovery program. The National Industrial Recovery Act (NIRA) was approved in 1933. Created by the act, the National Recovery Administration (NRA) developed codes of fair competition, maximum hours and minimum wages, according to industry. There was a guarantee that employees had the right to organize and bargain collectively through their chosen representatives.

The ACWA took advantage of the situation to organize the unorganized in men's clothing, cotton garments and the shirt workers. At the end of 1933, there were 50,000 new clothing workers. The ACWA so strongly believed that all clothing workers should be unionized that it actively recruited many members for the International Ladies' Garment Workers Union (ILGWU).

In 1935, the United States Supreme Court declared NIRA unconstitutional. However, later that year, the Wagner Labor Relations Act was favorable to unions. Company unions were outlawed; the act required employers to bargain in good faith with union representatives; and the National Labor Relations Board (NLRB) was created to monitor union-management relations.

Aware that more abuses than ever were taking place when work was so hard to get, ACWA concentrated on unionizing the "runaways," which employed many women. The drive began in 1933 and continued for several years. The work brought Bellanca to many states, including Tennessee and South Carolina. In Allentown, Pennsylvania, she persuaded Cornelia Pinchot, the governor's wife, to join her on the picket line.

Bellanca participated in a strike at Rochester, New York, in 1933. The pickets were peaceful, but city officials used first tear gas and then mounted police. The U.S. government finally intervened, and under the NRA, a solution satisfactory to the strikers was negotiated. An ACWA publicist wrote in the union publication *Advance*, "Dorothy is loved by the strikers, admired by the neighbors around the factories and feared by the police."

August Bellanca declined nomination to the General Executive Board in 1934 because of poor health. His wife was reelected to her former position, which she held until she died. She was its only female vice-president.

Bellanca was becoming very interested in politics. She belonged to the Labor Party, but supported both La Guardia, a Republican, and Roosevelt, a Democrat, because she believed that each helped the working person. In 1936, 1939 and 1944, she worked on Roosevelt's election campaigns. In 1938, she was the Congressional candidate from New York's 8th District on both the American Labor and Republican tickets. She failed to win election.

She held various non-union positions such as membership on Mayor Fiorella La Guardia's committee on unemployment, on Secretary of Labor Frances Perkins' advisory committee on maternal and child welfare, and on the women's policy committee of the War Manpower Commission. She worked with New York state agencies concerned with discrimination in employment and on a New York City committee to promote understanding among the city's ethnic groups. She attended numerous conferences. Bellanca opposed an Equal Rights Amendment (ERA) because she believed that the removal of protective legislation would not help working class women.

The Bellancas lived in Manhattan near the ACWA headquarters. They had successfully invested in Bellanca Aircraft Corporation, with which August's brother Giuseppe was connected. This provided additional income. The couple owned a country home in Ellenville, located in Ulster County in New York. Colleagues from the General Executive Board were often invited there.

By 1946, the ACWA membership had reached 350,000. This reflected the great influx of women into the work force during World War II. Bellanca realized that women would not be content to return home. According to her:

> Any realistic program for full employment must offer employment for all men and women who wish to work, irrespective of need. Planning on any other basis will not only fail to provide jobs for all those seeking jobs, but will waste a valuable human resource, the high skills which millions of women have attained in industry in the past years.

Dorothy Bellanca died of multiple myeloma, a malignant disease, in 1946 just after she reached 52. In her honor, ACWA endowed two beds in the children's ward at Memorial Hospital in New York City.

Today ACWA is part of UNITE!— Union of Needletrades, Industrial and Textile Employees.

Among the many tributes written to Dorothy Jacobs Bellanca, one from her friend, Mayor La Guardia, is very informative. In 1938, he said:

> Dorothy thinks straight. She is forceful in her expression, is devoted to her duties, is industrious and energetic and above all, has a soul. Dorothy Bellanca need not refer to statistics. She need not refer to shelves. She need not get her information from books. She knows the family life of the workers in the factory. She knows the ambitions of every family for their children. She typifies the spirit of America.

The immigrant child from Latvia had become the woman that typified the spirit of America.

Gerty Theresa
Radnitz Cori

In 1947, Gerty Cori and her husband Carl were awarded one half of the Nobel Prize for Medicine or Physiology. In that same year, she learned that she had a deadly disease. During the next ten years, as her health failed, she continued to do significant work.

Gerty Radnitz was born August 15, 1896, in Prague, then part of the Austro-Hungarian Monarchy. Her parents were Martha (Neustadt) Radnitz and Otto Radnitz. The latter was a chemist and businessman, the manager of several beet-sugar refineries. The Radnitz family, consisting of three daughters of whom Gerty was the oldest, was Jewish and lived in comfortable circumstances.

Radnitz was tutored at home until she was 10, then was sent to a private school for girls. Encouraged by an uncle who was a professor of pediatrics at the University of Prague, she decided to go to medical school. She lacked the necessary preparation in Latin, mathematics, physics and chemistry, but made up the deficiencies by studying hard and enrolling at a gymnasium, from which she graduated in 1914. (A gymnasium was a secondary school that prepared students for the university.) She passed what she always considered a very stiff examination to enter the medical school of the Carl Ferdinand University in Prague.

One of Radnitz's classmates was Carl Cori, the son of a zoologist who directed the Marine Biological Station in Trieste. The two studied together, took excursions to the countryside or went skiing. Radnitz was tall and slender, with reddish-brown hair and brown eyes; she was intelligent, vivacious, quick and aggressive, with a sense of humor. Cori, who was non–Jewish, was handsome, but shy and less likely to make an impression. The couple shared many interests besides science: outdoor life, literature, music and art, to name a few.

During the third year, Cori was drafted into the Austrian Army to fight in World War I. However, they graduated together in 1920. They were married that same year. Anti-Semitism was common, and Gerty converted to Catholicism.

It was a time of great hardship. Prague in 1918 had become the capital of Czechoslovakia. The Coris did manage to find jobs in Vienna — Gerty at the children's hospital and Carl at a clinic of the University of Vienna. Gerty's diet was so bad that she developed xerophthalmia, a condition of vitamin A deficiency. (Ironically, the Hoover relief organization had offered a dietary supplement, but the physicians had opted not to accept it.) At Carl's clinic, a free meal a day substituted for pay. At least the Coris were able to enjoy the culture of Vienna.

Although it had seemed likely that Gerty would become a pediatrician, by 1922 she and her husband had decided to pursue research careers rather than the practice of clinical medicine. Finding good research positions in Europe was unlikely at the time, and they were eager to get away. So eager in fact, that they had applied to the Dutch government to work for five years as physicians among the natives of Java.

A solution came before their applications were answered. In 1922, Carl was hired by the New York State Institute for the study of malignant disease — later the Roswell Park Memorial Institute of Buffalo — to run the hospital's clinical laboratory; he could devote his spare time to research of his own choosing.

Gerty arrived six months later and was assigned to the pathology department of the Institute. At this time, she and Carl began a long-lived collaboration on an investigation of carbohydrate metabolism and its regulation. (He later refused an offer that did not permit this.) They made a good team — both were ambitious, but never competed with each other; each trusted the other's work.

On the personal level, the Coris became Americanized during the Buffalo years. (They were naturalized in 1928.) They tried to learn the history, the politics and culture of their adopted country. They wanted to have some familiarity with American literature, and read aloud to each other. (As the years went by, Gerty specialized in history and biography; she was always a reader. Carl's taste was in poetry, art and archaeology.) They made friends with scientists and also with people in the world of music. They took in plays in New York City and spent vacations in the Adirondacks and Cape Cod. They were in Buffalo for nine years.

In 1931, Carl was offered the chairmanship of the pharmacology department at Washington University in St. Louis. By bending the university's nepotism rules, the administration was able to offer Gerty a research position in the same department. There was only a token salary.

Nepotism laws were common in those days, and with the Depression overshadowing everything, the Coris were lucky to find work. However, Gerty would remain "research associate" for 13 years — a position hardly commensurate with her abilities. In 1944, she became associate professor and was granted tenure. Three years later, Carl became chairman of the university's new biochemistry department. He promoted Gerty to full professor with a suitable salary as of July 1, 1947. During the 1950s, Washington University changed its nepotism rules, making it possible for husbands and wives to work there if they were in different departments. The chancellor wrote Gerty a personal letter to make it clear that the regulations were not aimed at her. She remained in Carl's department until her death.

In Buffalo, the Coris had studied the absorption of sugars, then the fate of ingested sugars. They used whole animals and were, no doubt, influenced by the work in the 1920s of Banting and Best on insulin and diabetes. Carl and Gerty also investigated the action of hormones that control carbohydrate metabolism.

Glycogen, sometimes called animal starch, is the storage form of glucose, the sugar that provides energy for the body. At Washington University, the Coris used tissue preparations to study specific chemical reactions that took place in the breakdown and buildup of glycogen. They were able to identify the enzymes, or catalysts, involved and to isolate intermediate products formed in the stepwise reactions. They succeeded in synthesizing glycogen in a test tube. This was later termed "one of the most brilliant achievements of modern biochemistry." They also elucidated the structure of glycogen.

The Coris work attracted to their laboratory talented and highly competent scientists from various parts of the world. Several of them would win Nobel prizes: Arthur Kornberg, Earl Sutherland, Edwin Krebs, Severo Ochoa, Christian de Duve and Luis Leloir. Gerty stood for perfection and everyone was aware of her high standards. She kept abreast of the literature in her field and was noted for her grasp of the subject matter. She worked extremely hard — even up to a short time before she delivered son Thomas in 1936. She was then 40. Thomas in time would earn a Ph.D. in chemistry.

The Coris enjoyed life in St. Louis. Guests at their home included not only scientists, but also artists, musicians, novelists and business people. Gerty and Carl skated, swam, played tennis, gardened and went to concerts. During their summer vacations, they went mountain climbing in the Rockies or the Alps. They sometimes went to Europe; one of Gerty's sisters, a painter, lived in Italy.

Carl and Gerty received many honors for their work, the greatest being the 1947 Nobel Prize for Physiology or Medicine, which was awarded jointly to them for their discovery of the process involved in the catalytic metabolism of glycogen, and to Bernardo Houssay of Argentina for his work on the role of the anterior pituitary hormone in the distribution of glycogen in the body and control of diabetes. The prize money amounted to about $25,000. This they shared with some coworkers on the phosphorylase project. The enzyme phosphorylase played a central part in their achievement. The coworkers who received a bonus were Sidney Colwick, Arda Green and Gerhard Schmidt.

The first American woman to win the Nobel prize in the category of medicine or physiology, Gerty Cori in 1953 made these candid statements:

> Certain general human drives are often of great intensity in scientists.
> 1. Curiosity, wanting to know. Knowing means bringing order out of chaos which is a deeply satisfying experience.
> 2. Wish to benefit man; knowledge is hoped to have beneficial results for humanity or at least for one's own nation.
> 3. Quest for fame and prestige, in short for power. These three ingredients are present in unequal amounts in each research worker. I am not sure whether preponderance of the third and basest has not sometimes led to great successes. Without a strong dose of the first, success becomes unlikely.

About the work that won the Nobel prize, Carl said, "Our efforts have been largely complementary, and one without the other would not have gone as far as in combination."

About the same time that the Coris learned of their greatest scientific recognition, they also learned that Gerty was seriously ill. While skiing in Colorado at 14,000 feet, she had fainted. The cause was later made clear — her hemoglobin level was too low to deliver sufficient oxygen to her brain. The diagnosis was agnogenic myeloid metaplasia. In

Gerty Theresa Cori, M.D.

Courtesy Archives, Washington University School of Medicine.

this rare and fatal condition, the bone marrow ceases to produce necessary cells of the blood, thus causing anemia. Gerty would be dependent on blood transfusions for the rest of her life.

She was determined to keep on working. Nobel Laureates in good health often find it difficult to do significant work, but Gerty let nothing deter her. Turning her attention to glycogen-storage disease (called von Gierke's disease, described in 1929), she demonstrated in 1952 that an enzyme named glucose-6-phosphatase was missing from the liver of a patient with the disease. This was the first demonstration of an inherited deficiency of a liver enzyme. Her work on glycogen storage disease continued, but her health was deteriorating.

The blood transfusions had side effects. During the period she was receiving them, much less was known about possible antigen-antibody reactions than is known today. Various palliative measures were tried, including removal of the spleen. But the progress of the disease was inexorable. She died of kidney failure on October 26, 1957, at the age of 61. She was at home, alone with Carl, who had given her strong support during her illness. Shortly before he died in 1984, he said to a friend, "You know, Gerty was heroic."

Gerty Radnitz Cori said this about her success: "I believe that the benefits of two civilizations, a European education followed by the freedom and opportunities of this country, have been essential to whatever contributions I have been able to make in science."

Eva Le Gallienne

A consummate actress, Eva Le Gallienne dedicated her talents to providing first-class theater at affordable prices. She encountered difficulties in obtaining financing for this endeavor, but her efforts brought pleasure to countless Americans of her day.

Eva was born in London on June 11, 1899. Her father, Richard Le Gallienne, was a poet and writer. Of Breton descent, he had added Le to his family name of Gallienne. Eva's mother was Julie (Norregaard), a Danish woman who became a correspondent for Denmark's newspaper *Politiken*. Richard's first wife had died and his grief was still acute when he remarried. According to Robert Schanke, Eva's biographer, their two-year marriage was heavily mired in debt, drinking and dalliance by the time Eva was born. Her father was a poor supporter, away often and drunk much of the time. Schanke noted that by age 2, Eva's life was filled with confusion, disruption and loneliness. By age 4, there was still no stability in her life: She and her adored nanny, Susan Stenning, moved to Paris to be with Julie. This caused separation from the half-sister she loved. Hesper, who was five years older, remained in England with an uncle. At the time, Eva's parents were separated, obtaining a divorce in 1911.

Julie's writing supported the household, so the nanny's offer to work for a year without recompense was most welcome. When *Politiken* refused some of Julie's articles, thereby cutting down her income, she opened a millinery shop.

At 3, Eva had seen the dramatization of *The Water Babies*. At 7, she watched Sarah Bernhardt play the lead in *The Sleeping Beauty*. Eva sometimes performed on her own, without her mother's knowledge: At a busy crosswalk in the Bois de Boulogne she sang Danish and German folk songs as well as favorites from the English music hall. Her straw hat, used as a collection box, once received as much as five francs.

At 8, Eva was sent to the Collège Sevigne, which prepared girls for France's celebrated Sorbonne. She felt at home in the school's academic atmosphere and remained there for five years.

During that period, she usually spent Christmas in Copenhagen with Julie's family. Through these relatives, Eva became interested in Hans Christian Andersen. Sometimes she was taken to the Royal Theater, of which she was given a free replica. For that model, she designed special scenery for the plays she had seen; she created footlights and provided for special effects such as rain.

Summer vacations allowed her to return to England. When Hesper visited, the girls acted out scenes from *As You Like It* and *Romeo and Juliet*. When she was 12, Eva took lessons in acting from London actress Constance Collier, who quickly recognized the young girl's extraordinary talent.

In 1911, Le Gallienne attended an English boarding school, which she disliked because it lacked the standards of her previous school. Her boredom was relieved by spending Christmas in Paris with her mother.

Le Gallienne's interest in the theater was further whetted by seeing Sarah Bernhardt perform in several productions, including *La Dame aux Camelias*, *La Reine Elizabeth* and *Phèdre*. So great was her interest that she once copied in longhand Bernhardt's 800-page *Memoirs*—she had no money to buy the book. She met the "divine" Bernhardt for the first time in 1913 when her mother took her backstage, as was prearranged.

Thanks to Constance Collier, her acting tutor, Le Gallienne made her professional debut in 1914 at a matinee performance of *Manna Vanna* by Maeterlinck, the Belgian playwright.

The budding actress had plans to study theater in Munich. A family friend anticipated the war that was to come and offered to help finance her training in London at Herbert Beerbohm Tree's Academy (later the Royal Academy of Dramatic Art). She attended for two terms, her program including dancing, fencing, voice production, elocution and Delsarte.

Cast as a rough-spoken cockney in one of the academy's plays, she did so well that she was offered the part of a cockney maid in *The Laughter of Fools*. That performance led to several offers. Of significant importance to her was the possibility that David Belasco would produce *The Laughter of Fools* on Broadway. With that in mind, in August 1915, Le Gallienne and her mother took ship for New York.

It turned out that Belasco decided against producing the play, leaving

Le Gallienne with no work in sight. In late September, she was chosen to play a Negro maid in *Mrs. Boltray's Daughter,* a Broadway production. The show ran for 17 performances — and then she was out of work again.

She looked for parts and read Ibsen in her free time. She made a list of the plays she intended to do before reaching 35. These masterpieces included *Hedda Gabler, The Master Builder, Peter Pan, La Dame aux Camelias, Romeo and Juliet* and *L'Aiglon.*

Nevertheless, her next role was in a play less ambitious for her than those on the list —*Bunny*— and it offered another cockney character. The show played in Elmira, Rochester and Syracuse.

Le Gallienne earned a supporting role in *Mr. Lazarus,* which opened in Washington, D.C. It then had a summer run in Chicago, and her acting received great accolades. Before the scheduled New York opening, the playwrights came to watch a performance. They noted that Le Gallienne was overplaying her role; she, however, refused to change her presentation.

Her next offer was from Oliver Morosco. As the lead in this new play, Le Gallienne had rehearsed under director Robert Milton. Morosco was present at the final dress rehearsal, and made significant changes. Le Gallienne did not agree with his ideas. The upshot was that she was fired. That incident on the heels of her attitude about *Lazarus* was bad news for her career. The Broadway establishment labeled her as uncooperative and barely directable. For the next four years, Le Gallienne had no major roles on the New York stage; she had to take what she could on the road. During this time she had the good fortune to act with and learn from Ethel Barrymore.

Le Gallienne had previously turned down an offer from David Belasco, the producer so greatly admired by Mary Pickford. Le Gallienne realized that he would insist on absolute loyalty, and she knew herself well enough to realize that she would not always agree with him.

After five years in the United States, Le Gallienne finally attained star status. In 1920, she received good reviews as the leading lady in Arthur Richman's *Not So Long Ago.* After the second performance, the Schuberts offered her a three-year contract, without specific assignments, at $250 a week — a considerable salary for that day. She was now supporting her mother, who had moved back to London, so money had to be considered.

The Schuberts graciously released her to do Julie in a Theater Guild production of *Liliom,* playing opposite Joseph Schildkraut. Le Gallienne quarreled with the director, not merely demanding, but getting, freedom to direct herself. Also, she and Schildkraut had personality clashes. Nevertheless, she got rave reviews, and the production had a long run. After it closed on Broadway, it was scheduled for a summer 1922 run in Chicago. Unfortunately, after a few weeks, Le Gallienne collapsed from the strain.

After recovery, she visited Europe, accepting an invitation to Budapest via Paris, Genoa, Venice, Munich and Vienna. In Budapest she was honored by Ferene Molnar, the revered author of *Liliom*.

Le Gallienne's next important part was in *The Swan*, another play by Molnar. Billie Burke, the highly popular wife of Florenz Ziegfeld, was being considered for the part, but Molnar insisted on Le Gallienne.

Before rehearsals for *The Swan* started, Le Gallienne had time for another trip to Europe. In London, she had the opportunity to observe the great Italian-born actress Eleanora Duse in *Cosi Sia*. That experience convinced her that Duse, not Bernhardt, was the world's greatest actress. Later she saw Duse in Ibsen's magnificent *Ghosts*; she also exchanged ides and talked with her on several occasions.

The Swan brought Le Gallienne even more praise than *Liliom*. It ran until July 1924, then toured until 1925. However, one critic wrote in *Theater Magazine*: "Miss Le Gallienne seldom rings true in scenes where she is called upon to reciprocate masculine ardor."

Although Le Gallienne resented that fact that some critics referred to her acting as "cold and intellectual," she believed that she had won her spurs with regard to Broadway. For some time it had been her dream to give the American theater what was familiar to her in Paris, Copenhagen and other European cities: the best, at the lowest possible rate, and to present plays in repertory companies. "The kind of theater I wanted to play in didn't exist in this country, so it seemed quite natural to try to create one," she said.

Le Gallienne gave up much of the glamour and higher pay of Broadway, which were not particularly important to her. She was a beautiful woman, but unlike many other performers with star billing, insisted on wearing whatever was most suitable for the part, whether it became her or not. Le Gallienne's dedication to the theater was such that she was even willing to give the public what she thought it needed, not necessarily what she thought it wanted.

In 1925, she chose first two Ibsen plays, *The Master Builder* and *John Gabriel Borkman*, starring in her own productions. After successful Broadway performances, she took them on a spring tour of eastern cities. As a producer, Le Gallienne was involved in many aspects besides acting — play selection, casting, costumes, lighting, blocking and so on. She was a strong-minded woman with ideas and not given to backing down.

By 1926, Le Gallienne had formed the Civic Repertory Theatre. It was a subsidized operation, and, according to her, no rich person was safe in her presence. She was predatory and ruthless, and admitted her "Robin Hood tactics with various wealthy patrons." A building in New York City on 14th Street between 6th and 7th avenues was purchased. First opened in 1866 as the French Theater, it served the purposes of the new endeavor.

The first production of the theater was *Saturday Night*, presented in October 1926. Over six seasons, there were 1,581 performances of 34 different plays — both classical and modern. The list included such outstanding works as *The Three Sisters, Twelfth Night, Hedda Gabler, The Cherry Orchard, Romeo and Juliet, Camille* and *Alice in Wonderland*. Le Gallienne herself starred in and directed all but two of the productions.

Romeo and Juliet was one of the most popular, a critic noting: "This is a Juliet well acquainted with the facts of life and the persuasions of love." This was certainly an improvement over the review in *Theater Magazine* of her *Swan* performance.

Peter Pan was a special favorite of children. The 129 performances included one free, annual Christmas matinee for orphans and underprivileged children. As Peter, Le Gallienne wore blue leotards, blue suede sandals and a blue jerkin trimmed with green leaves. For her curtain call, she "flew" (in a harness on wires) to the second balcony. On one occasion, a child went backstage to let her know that he had discovered how she was able to fly: "You take a big swallow of gas and then you go up in the air like a balloon!"

The version chosen for *Alice in Wonderland* used Sir John Tenniel's illustrations and a score composed by Richard Addinsell of "Warsaw Concerto" fame.

The Civic Repertory Theatre brought Le Gallienne many honors and increased recognition such as her photo on the cover of *Time* for November 25, 1929. She was embarrassed by eulogies about her great sacrifice and unselfish devotion to the theater. In her own words, "I felt lucky to be doing what I wanted!"

Le Gallienne had planned a respite after the theater's first five years. Since 1926 she had had a small house in Weston, Connecticut. It was more than 200 years old and situated on about four acres of rocky woodland.

Later she bought more land and built on it. There, among trees, flowers and the animals that she loved, she had retreated to rest in 1931.

A month later, a propane gas explosion in her cellar almost killed her. She was in critical condition for more than a week. A long convalescence followed. Both hands were seriously affected, the right one in particular; her face was burned. As soon as she was able to travel, she sailed for Europe. In Paris, she took fencing lessons to strengthen her wrist and hand. Several operations were eventually necessary. Many years later she wrote that this accident, which at the time appeared so tragic and bitter, taught her much about selfishness, vanity, ruthlessness and personal ambition.

While in Paris, Le Gallienne worked for a short time in a circus under an assumed name. She claimed that there she learned much that improved her acting. She resigned from this position before her mother arrived from England for a visit.

The Civic Repertory Theatre opened again in the fall of 1932, as planned, continuing until the middle of May. Le Gallienne was finding it increasingly difficult to meet expenses as the effects of the Depression spread. She decided on an extensive tour to last through the spring of 1934.

Eleanor Roosevelt had seen *Alice* in Washington, D.C. Through the First Lady, Le Gallienne was invited to the White House to talk with President Franklin Roosevelt about financial aid from the government. FDR wanted to expand the WPA to the theater as a means of providing employment; there would be no consideration of talent. In contrast, the subsidized state theaters of Europe — the Comedie Française and the Moscow Art Theater, for example — demanded the highest standards. These were Le Gallienne's models, and she found Roosevelt's idea unacceptable. As a result of the conversation, she dropped any hope of obtaining government subsidy. It was her belief that great talent would surface; according to her thinking, there were no "mute inglorious Miltons" such as described in Gray's "Elegy Written in a Country Churchyard."

Nevertheless, she continued to insist on low admission prices and the repertory concept. Another problem was that most first-rate actors and actresses preferred to act on Broadway. In addition, American playwrights could make more money when their works ran for long periods on Broadway rather than as part of a repertory project.

For all these reasons, the Civic Repertory Theatre, laudable as in was, ended officially in 1936, with the last two years falling far below Le Gallienne's expectations.

Eva Le Gallienne

Eva Le Gallienne in Hedda Gabler. *Photograph by Talbot. Courtesy Museum of the City of New York.*

After the demise of the theater, Le Gallienne found a role that she had long been interested in — Hamlet. The play opened at the Cape Playhouse in Dennis, Massachusetts. One New York critic was not impressed with her, while one from Boston rated her portrayal as "a rival to Bernhardt." Lee Schubert wanted a limited Broadway engagement.

Le Gallienne declined, fearing too much criticism of a female Hamlet plus comparison to the recent, then contemporary, performances of British actors John Gielgud and Leslie Howard. Le Gallienne also genuinely disliked the prospect of playing the same part night after night.

Since money was a problem, Le Gallienne could not afford to be too selective. She even went on tour with a vaudeville act. During most of the 1940-41 season, she was reduced to lecturing tours for universities and women's clubs. A stint as director with the Theater Guild followed.

During the 1945-46 season, Le Gallienne again tried to establish a new permanent organization called the American Repertory Theatre. She was joined by Margaret Webster, the daughter of Dame May Whitty, and Cheryl Crawford, who had been associated with the Theater Guild and was an experienced director. In the beginning, they worked indefatigably to promote their venture to clubs and organizations in several eastern states. They issued brochures and spoke on radio programs — sometimes even on nationwide broadcasts. They managed to sell stock worth $300,000. Some of their sponsors were William Paley, Mrs. Ephraim Zimbalist, Katherine Cornell, Carl Van Dorn, Helen Hayes, Fredric March, Mary Martin and Jo Mielziner. This new repertory group opened with *Henry VIII*.

After a year, it was clear that the experiment would fail. For instance, budgets were excessive and there were untoward expenses because of union regulations. To exemplify the latter, one production required 28 stagehands, which meant that all the rest had to have 28 stagehands even if only 10 were needed. An appeal to John D. Rockefeller failed. Even Margaret Webster and Le Gallienne offered to work without salary, to no avail. After Ibsen's famed *Hedda Gabler* closed, the American Repertory Theatre Corporation was dissolved in 1948 with a loss of $340,000.

Following the second failure of her professional dream, Le Gallienne was in more or less semi-retirement for the next six years.

In 1949, her *Flossie and Bessie* was published by Harper. This literary work concerned two bantam hens from her farm and was considered a children's book. According to its author, though, it was a satire about her own situation. Faber and Faber produced a British edition the following year. They returned to the title that Harper and Harper had rejected: *A Moral Tale*.

Le Gallienne earned some money with national lecture tours, speaking about great plays and giving selected scenes. She also had a radio show on which she read stories and scenes from plays. She made translations of Ibsen plays and wrote corresponding prefaces; by 1961, Modern Library had published 12.

She did a summer tour, playing with great success Miss Moffat in *The Corn Is Green.*

Soon afterwards, Hesper and her husband moved from England to Connecticut. The half-sisters had not seen one another for decades, and now they would be living within ten miles of each other.

In 1952, Le Gallienne, Margaret Webster and Maurice Evans founded Theatre Masterworks. Since it was committed to recording a library of plays not popular with the commercial theater, she considered this second best to a repertory theater. Her own contributions included recordings from *Hedda Gabler,* from *An Evening with Will Shakespeare* and her recording of some outstanding English and American poetry.

A year later, she toured California, reciting two of Oscar Wilde's stories. This required the incredible memorization of 57 pages of prose — a task she was proud of accomplishing at 54.

Le Gallienne became associated with Westport's highly regarded White Barn Theater in 1955. Here she taught acting in the summer. One of her students was Peter Falk, who 30 years later wrote to her, "I'll always be indebted to you." She thoroughly enjoyed this venture and often invited her classes to her home. The loved to hear her talk about Duse and Bernhardt.

Finally there was an opportunity for Le Gallienne to reclaim her acting reputation — as Queen Elizabeth in *Mary Stuart.* (The first choice was Judith Anderson, who refused because the salary was not high enough.) Her performance at the off–Broadway Phoenix Theater was a huge success — one viewer observed, "She became Elizabeth!" Eventually the play went on tour; another bonus was that Le Gallienne was awarded the title role in *Elizabeth the Queen.*

More offers came. In 1958, she appeared on television in three dramatic specials with other stage luminaries. A *New York Times* reviewer noted that millions of viewers watched "acting at its supreme best."

After her role as Elizabeth, Le Gallienne toured when the same company produced *Ghosts* in 1962. Again she directed and starred. Reviewers were ecstatic. Then for three years she was on the road. Tours were not easy, and during her lifetime she did not escape some of the hazards. With a house sold out, she once learned an hour and a half before curtain time that the actress playing Mrs. Malaprop in *The Rivals* was in the hospital. With no adequate understudy on hand, Le Gallienne

played the part. With the help of a prompter from the wings and cue-
ing when she went offstage, she was able to please the audience. Another
time, a boxcar containing sets had been switched with one belonging
to a Ringling Brothers circus. When the car thought to contain Elizabeth's throne was opened, out came an elephant. (The throne was flown
in, with a 15-minute delay in curtain time.)

In 1966, Le Gallienne received kudos for the biography she wrote
of Eleanora Duse.

After a heart attack in 1968, Le Gallienne had more time to enjoy
her Connecticut home. She also published a translation of *The Little
Mermaid*, a review of two biographies of Ibsen and an article on Sarah
Bernhardt. She even took a part in *All's Well That Ends Well*.

In 1972, Le Gallienne tried to interest the author of a novel entitled *The Dream Watcher* in dramatizing it. Barbara Werba did produce
a play from her book. Three years later, Lucille Lortel decided to present that play at the White Barn. Le Gallienne was given the part of an
80-year-old woman who befriends a young boy. One reviewer described
her performance as flawless.

A week later, she was offered the lead in *The Royal Family*, to be
produced at Kennedy Center. It proved so successful that it went on
national tour for 1976-77.

A curious example of Le Gallienne's capacity to affect others —
wittingly or unwittingly — follows. A man named Frank Sager of Glendale, California, died in 1978. He left his estate of $55,000 to her. She
had never met him, but he described her as "the woman I love."

At age 80, Le Gallienne acted in a movie called *Resurrection*. It was
filmed in Texas and the shooting required three weeks. Ever the per-
former, she had hired a voice coach to teach her the rural Georgia dialect
required for her part, and she did remember her lines.

Her next appearance was in *To Grandmother's House We Go*. It
opened on January 14, 1981, with good reviews for her acting. When
her voice could not be heard, she was "miked"— against her will and
knowledge.

Sadly, Le Gallienne's attempt to direct *Alice in Wonderland* to honor
its 50th anniversary was a failure.

With an inheritance of more than $1 million from a friend named
Alice De Lamar, Le Gallienne gained financial security when her life
was almost over.

Her final role was in the *St. Elsewhere* television series. She could
no longer remember lines and had to read them from hidden cue cards.

Although she spent her last days tending her garden, looking after her animals and even doing carpentry, she was lonesome, for most of those near and dear to her had died. Her secretary noted that the great Le Gallienne's memory was failing.

When invited to the White House to receive the National Medal of the Arts, to be presented by President Reagan, she sent a representative to receive the medal — the highest honor to be bestowed on an artist by the government of the United States.

She died on June 3, 1991, at the age of 92.

Eva Le Gallienne was influenced by European culture, which in various ways, she imported to her adopted country; to illustrate, through her efforts, the works of Ibsen, Chekov and Hans Christian Andersen became better known and understood. (To recognize her Ibsen translations, the King of Norway awarded her the Cross of the Royal Order of St. Olaf, the highest honor granted a foreigner.)

Le Gallienne wrote two autobiographies —*At 33*, published in 1935, and *With a Quiet Heart*, published 20 years later. Robert Schanke, an authority on theater and author of her 1992 biography, was critical that she failed to mention she had lesbian relationships with several partners and also that she was an alcoholic. He pointed out that she was often uncooperative, arrogant, insensitive, ruthless and disinclined to come to the defense of colleagues accused of being Communists. Critical as he was of her faults, his admiration of her as a professional actress is immense. And rightly so.

Epilogue

It is of interest to examine from a variety of perspectives the accomplishments of the 15 women who are the subjects of this book.

From the fact that they were immigrants we can infer that they or their parents were adventuresome enough to seek a better life or better opportunities in what was to them a foreign land.

Family influence varied considerably. Elizabeth Blackwell's enlightened father believed in equality of education for boys and girls. Lilly Spencer's parents actively encouraged her talent. Both the father and mother of Senda Berenson stressed the value of education. Adelaide Nutting's mother saw to it that her children were well instructed, even if this entailed sacrifice. Ernestine Schumann-Heink had a mother who maintained faith in her daughter's great talent — in spite of her husband's disagreement. Mary Pickford was unusually dependent on her mother, although her mother's financial security depended on Pickford. Eva Le Gallienne owed much, materially and professionally, to her mother, whose husband had left her. Evangeline Booth had both parents to look up to as role models. The memory of her mother's struggle to help her children was the basis of Dorothy Loeb's crusade to aid widowed mothers. An older sister played a pivotal part in the raising of Francesca Cabrini. Adelaide Nutting was very close to a sister. A career in medicine was suggested for Gerty Cori by an uncle, while Maria Kraus-Boelté's aunt recommended that her niece learn Froebel's methods.

Ambition manifested itself in Spencer, Shaw, Schumann-Heink, Pickford, Rubinstein and Le Gallienne. Ambition may not be the correct word to apply to Cabrini and Booth, but both showed great determination to rise in their chosen callings. Although Shaw was ambitious, she was willing to step aside when she deemed it expedient. Loeb, in contrast to the ambitious, appeared to be selfless with regard to social action.

Today, a college education is considered one of the keys to success, although undue emphasis is probably placed on a degree. Yet only Blackwell, Shaw and Cori had post-secondary training. Bellanca and Pickford in particular had very sketchy educations. Shaw, living in the wilderness, found that she knew more than her teacher, but the education that she picked up enabled her to earn two advanced degrees. On the other hand, two of the women — Rubinstein and Cori — were the products of the renowned European gymnasium education. Nutting held no degree, but was highly educated through reading and travel; the same could be said of Le Gallienne. It appears that each woman learned — one way or another — what she needed. Currently, life is so structured that similar feats by modern women would probably not be possible without formal educational accreditation.

Luck — good or bad — is an element that enters into life's transactions. For some of the women, the time was right: Shaw's preaching ability gained recognition through the suffragist cause; the migration of countless Italians to the United States came at an opportune time to utilize the talents of Cabrini; men's basketball was invented at the right time in Senda Berenson's career for her to promote the girls' game; Mary Pickford, as a stage actress, was lured by the movies as they surpassed stage plays in popularity; during a terrible war, Booth saw new opportunity for the Salvation Army to be of service. But the Depression was not the right time for Eva Le Gallienne's laudable project to flourish. And sometimes luck comes in the form of considered action, as when Schumann-Heink was given voice lessons *gratis*.

A strong commitment to religion in the home often has impact on the children. This was so in the lives of Cabrini and Booth. Blackwell remained devout all her life. Pickford, a Catholic, turned to the Christian Science church. Although Shaw was an ordained minister, one gains the impression that she was more interested in the suffragist cause than in the church. One third of the women were Jewish — Berenson, Rubinstein, Loeb, Bellanca and Cori — but apparently religion did not dominate their lives. It can be concluded that the outlook of the majority of the 15 was secular rather than religious.

Talent or ability is obviously a prime factor in success. Spencer had artistic talent; Schumann-Heink was blessed with an exceptional voice; Rubinstein had rare financial acumen. Pickford and Le Gallienne were endowed with dramatic talent. Cori, Shaw and Blackwell had intellectual ability. The ability to organize was especially marked in Cabrini and Booth, and to a lesser extent in Bellanca, Kraus-Boelté, Nutting,

Berenson and Loeb. Loeb put her journalistic skill to work for social reforms. Shaw used her oratorical ability on behalf of the suffragettes; Booth used her musical ability as she sought to save souls — and so on. Each woman had an ability pertinent to what she sought to accomplish, and some had more than one gift.

Some of their coping mechanisms are apparent. Cabrini drew strength from God. Booth, too, depended on religion. Blackwell and Loeb had faith that they were taking the right course. The wonders of nature afforded relaxation to Le Gallienne, while collecting art appeared to do the same for Rubinstein. Nutting and Cori were readers.

What of discrimination? These were women and immigrants. As women entering male-dominated professions, Blackwell and Shaw encountered it. Cori met it in the academic world; Bellanca fought it in the men's unions. However, for most of the 15 women, it appears that discrimination played a surprisingly small part. It may be argued that these particular women were not so aware of it as are women today.

Motivation becomes imperative when difficulties or roadblocks present themselves. Ambition played a role here, and noted previously were those women who were unusually ambitious. Economics played a major part in the motivation of some. For many years, the Pickford family depended on Mary's success; this did not lessen her ambition, but being the family's support certainly did much to motivate her performance. Schumann-Heink knew want in her youth, and later in her career she became the financial mainstay of her children. Rubinstein, young and on her own in the foreign land of Australia, had to succeed in order to eat. Having been forced to leave school to work in a factory, Bellanca set out at an exceptionally young age to improve working conditions for herself and other garment workers.

Until 1920, feminism's great goal was to make it legal for women to vote. With that accomplished — with effective aid from Shaw — feminists changed their sites. It is illuminating to consider how some of the 15 reacted to current standards of feminism. Spencer had modern ideas; she had a successful career plus a happy marriage and home life thanks to her husband's care of their children while she supported them all. Schumann-Heink stated publicly that she regarded her children and her art as equal. At the same time, she believed that women's influence in politics should be through their husbands. Also, despite her exalted standing in the world of opera, Schumann-Heink felt that she needed the support (non-financial) of a third husband. Blackwell fought successfully for opening the medical profession to women, but dissociated herself from the performance of abortions. It is true that the procedure was dangerous because of the high probability of infection and hemorrhage; nevertheless, one is left with the impression that her chief objection was a moral one. Blackwell also regarded marriage and her career as incompatible. Loeb, too, believed it essential for a mother to remain at home — not at work outside the home — with her children. Berenson did not support the ERA of her day. Much of the foregoing merely reinforces the often-disregarded caution that historic facts should be judged in the context of the standards of their time.

Six of the 15 women did not marry: Blackwell, Shaw, Cabrini, Nutting, Booth and Le Gallienne. Loeb, Schumann-Heink, Rubinstein and Pickford divorced; of these four, all but Loeb remarried. Only Spencer, Schumann-Heink, Rubinstein and Cori had children. Blackwell, Kraus-Boelté, Booth and Pickford adopted youngsters. (Shaw hoped to adopt a specific child, but was not successful.) The women who were without offspring, biological or otherwise, were Shaw, Cabrini, Nutting, Berenson, Loeb, Bellanca and Le Gallienne. This represents more than half the sample. We should also note that relatively late in their careers, Cori had her only child, while Kraus-Boelté and Pickford adopted one and two, respectively. Thus it appears that the majority of the women studied did not wish — for whatever reasons — to mix careers and children.

The modern world equates money with power. Some of these women had enviable records as financial managers. Rubinstein is the outstanding example of this, followed by Pickford. Cabrini and Booth, without seeking personal gain, found ingenious ways to support their charitable projects. Spencer was highly successful in earning money through her art. Le Gallienne, on the other hand, died with little money earned by herself. The others departed in apparently comfortable circumstances.

As immigrants, they were all loyal to the United States, although not all became citizens. Cori, Schumann-Heink, Booth and Berenson seemed especially appreciative of this country's opportunities. Blackwell apparently was more at home in her native England. The cosmopolitan Rubinstein and Le Gallienne probably would have thrived in a number of cultures. On reading Shaw's orations, one is led to consider her outlook so American, it is difficult to think of her as foreign-born. That Europe continued to have an important effect on the nation's culture is reflected by the travels to that continent by Blackwell, Nutting and Loeb. Considering that commercial air travel was not common until after World War II, the many voyages made to Europe by most of the 15 is surprising.

These women lived in an age when life expectancy was shorter than it is today, yet only four of them failed to reach the allotted Biblical three score years and ten: Cabrini, Loeb, Bellanca and Cori. Rubinstein died (in harness) at 94, Le Gallienne at 92; there were six octogenarians: Blackwell, Nutting, Pickford, Berenson, Booth and Kraus-Boelté. The three remaining died in their 70s: Spencer, Shaw and Schumann-Heink. At least, these women were all survivors; at best, their record was truly remarkable.

A person's place in history is difficult to assess because much depends on the time at which the observation is made. As we approach the end of the 20th century, these thoughts are in regard to each woman's position.

Elizabeth Blackwell's graduation from medical school was extremely important because other women would follow her example. In addition, she showed wisdom by seeing to it that her colleagues could not be accused of being quacks since she promoted high standards for women in the medical profession. She ultimately gained the respect of male practitioners.

Lilly Martin Spencer's art is little known today. Whether or not it will have a revival is a matter of speculation. Judging particularly by the number of lithographs of her works, people of her day liked what she produced.

Kraus-Boelté, as a disciple of Froebel, established the latter's system in the United States. Today it is unfamiliar to many, but it was once an innovation. Methods in education come and go, but there is now almost universal acceptance of the idea that preschool education is valuable — for example, the Head Start program has been popular for many years.

Anna Howard Shaw's great gift was oratory. This is still important, but what endures historically is the literary content of the oration, exemplified by such works as Lincoln's second inaugural address, Churchill's wartime speeches and Martin Luther King, Jr.'s "I Have a Dream" speech. Shaw's speeches would not rank with these examples, but her political oratory and her dedication to women's suffrage played an important part in bringing about the passage of the 19th Amendment. This is how she is remembered.

The U.S. immigrant population has changed greatly since Francesca Cabrini's "daughters" served numerous countrymen of hers and theirs who had immigrated to the United States. The issue of immigration itself is under constant attack; there is criticism that illegal immigration is often condoned. Despite all this, the Missionary Sisters of the Sacred Heart of Jesus continue to minister in the spirit of their founder, finding ways to be of assistance in a changed world.

Nursing education has become university-based rather than hospital-based, as Adelaide Nutting intended it to be. As the cost of medical care rises, there is pressure to use well-trained nurses for some tasks usually designated for physicians. This and other trends indicate that there is little likelihood that the training of nurses will return to hospitals.

Opera remains an important facet of American culture. The popularity of stars change, but Mme. Schumann-Heink's name ranks with the greatest of the Metropolitan Opera Association.

Ever since Franklin Roosevelt's New Deal, there has been some tendency for the public to count more on the government and less on private organizations to dispense charity. However, the American Salvation Army, strengthened by the long tenure of Evangeline Booth, remains strong and endorsed by the public.

Girls' basketball is still very popular with those who play it, and more and more, the game has become a spectator sport. The first aspect would please Senda Berenson, but what has become the competitive nature of the game would probably not meet with her approval. Nevertheless, competition is an important part of modern life, and women must be prepared to compete with one another and also with men.

At the time of this writing, Helena Rubinstein products are not sold in this country. They pleased women for many years before the line was discontinued. The money they brought in for so long is well invested, and through the oversight of the Helena Rubinstein Foundation, at present underwrites many worthy projects.

It is recognized that reactions to problems that arose in connection with orphanages originally spurred the modern social welfare system, and Sophie Irene Loeb was one of those who vehemently opposed orphanages. Now it is known that a few such institutions survived the extreme criticism and managed to do a fair job with their charges. According to McKenzie, they "appear to have known how to break the cycles of poverty, neglect and abuse for hordes of children." The problem of finding the best situation for an abused and deprived child is very complex and not likely to be solved to everyone's satisfaction.

As "America's Sweetheart," Mary Pickford enjoyed immense popularity for a long period. But tastes changed, and the sweet child/woman character that she represented has little in common with the television stars that reign today. This, of course, does not detract from Pickford's acting ability.

The power of unions waxes and wanes, but they seem destined to stay. It is clear that with regard to Dorothy Bellanca's garment industry, constant surveillance is needed to ensure that workers from foreign countries are not exploited and forced to work under sweat-shop conditions or worse. Bellanca was most perceptive when she observed that women, after World War II employment, would not willingly return to the home. It is still often assumed that married women work because their earnings are needed by their families. Bellanca stated that they would work, whether or not it was an economic necessity to do so. Modern women want to fulfill themselves, and many seem unable to do so through home and family.

As the first American woman to be awarded the Nobel Prize for Medicine or Physiology, Gerty Cori remains a role model for women scientists in the United States. (Other American women have been so honored since 1957.)

Eva Le Gallienne's standing is unique. She obtained stardom of first rank. Then, disregarding fame and financial gain, she embarked on a project dear to her heart — to bring European culture in the form of great drama to the common man. She had some success, but nothing permanent. Currently, the cost of theater tickets to good productions is still beyond the means of most Americans. While many who care for drama watch televised theater productions, this probably does not please all. No doubt Le Gallienne would rejoice to know that Ibsen and Chekhov are popular today; in fact, Nora of *A Doll's House* is a heroine of feminist literature.

What of the powers of endurance of these women? Did they, as Marilyn vos Savant put it, try hard enough? Did they give up too soon?

Blackwell's commitment was unrelenting. Facing hurdles to entrance to a medical school was an ordeal in itself, but after graduation, she encountered in practice more hostility from males and females alike. But she prevailed, and soon other women found a less arduous path to acceptance in the healing profession.

Spencer wanted to be a painter, and she pursued a serious course to that end. She was fortunate enough to have a successful career, children and an unbroken marriage.

Kraus-Boelté could presumably have led an easy and comfortable life without the burdens of a career. Such a course was the norm for the society she represented. Having been exposed to a happy preschool experience herself, she was convinced of the soundness of Froebel's concepts, and she saw an opportunity for many children to benefit from them. So for many years she worked hard and successfully to see that this happened.

A rugged character distinguished Shaw. There was much to deter her from obtaining a high school education, yet she went to college, theological school and medical school. Women ministers and women orators were not common in her day, but she functioned successfully as each. Above all, in spite of ups and downs, her commitment to the suffragist cause remained steadfast.

Cabrini intended to be a missionary. She had hoped to go to China, but the Holy Father had indicated that she and her nuns were needed in the West. She had a deep conviction that with divine guidance, anything was possible. Thus her courage never flagged, even when, for example, the band learned that a mistake had been made in urging them to come to the United States. They had no thought of leaving, as was suggested, and soon they were making themselves known here through countless good works.

Nutting was an indefatigable worker. She systematically thought out her course. When her vision took time for realization, she was patient. And she never gave up.

Aware that she possessed unusual talent, Schumann-Heink had high aspirations. She was undeterred by hardships such as poverty, a growing family and a perceived lack of good looks. When her inability to sight-read music threatened her career, she remedied the situation. She tried not to allow her personal life to affect her professional obligations.

For as long as she could remember, Booth was part of the Salvation Army. With her several talents, she would probably have done well in other professions or as wife and mother. But her commitment was to continue the work of her father and mother. This she did remarkably well and with constancy.

As a sickly young woman, Berenson had an intense dislike for the physical exercise program prescribed for her. But she did not give up; she worked as directed. To her pleasant surprise, she found benefit from the regimen. As a result, she devoted her efforts to physical education for girls, a relatively new endeavor at the time. And she was very successful.

Rubinstein left home because she refused to follow her father's wishes. She saw a way to support herself, and she did not spare herself in making her ideas work. She was so successful that she was soon on her way to earning a fortune. She was still working hard at the time of her death.

As a divorced woman, Loeb had to support herself—which she did as a journalist. She also committed herself to the cause of obtaining pensions for widowed mothers. This latter activity was not lucrative, but her commitment to that and related causes never wavered as long as she lived.

Pickford's resolve to advance as an actress is remarkable. As a child, she had parts in stage plays. As a young woman, she realized her goal of becoming the first lady of the screen. She worked hard all of her professional life, her career encompassing production as well as acting. Fortunately, she enjoyed what she did.

Bellanca believed in what she was doing, and never turned back. Over the years, she expended unceasing effort to educate workers about the benefits of unionization. Both as a young girl and a mature woman, she appeared on the picket line—a deed that must have required courage when unions were less popular and less protected by law.

Cori showed her determination at an early age by obtaining, despite inadequacies in her preparation, the gymnasium education required for medical school. Later, she and Carl decided to collaborate in their research. They kept this agreement in spite of a tempting offer to Carl that did not include his wife. Gerty worked for many years in an inferior position at Washington University; however, in so doing, she was able to produce, with Carl, the work that ultimately brought them their Nobel prize.

It seems unlikely that Le Gallienne even seriously considered a career other than the stage. Apparently unimpressed by directors or playwrights, she went her own way, playing the roles she aspired to, to become a leading actress. Even a serious accident failed to stop her acting. Despite setbacks, she persisted in promoting the concept of repertory theater at a low cost to the audience.

Two characteristics common to the 15 emerge: ability and perseverance. These attributes appear to be the keystones that made possible their rich contributions to the United States.

One of Sophie Loeb's *Epigrams of Eve* remains a guide to able women of future generations: "Do the thing you think is best, and abide by it like a soldier."

Sources

Aborn, Caroline D., et al. *Pioneers of the Kindergarten in America.* New York: Century, 1924.

Armstrong, William. *The Romantic World of Music.* New York: Dutton, 1922.

Asher, Nina L. *Dorothy Jacobs Bellanca: Feminist Trade Unionist, 1894–1946.* Ph.D. thesis. Ann Arbor, MI: University Microfilms International, 1983.

Berenson, Senda. *Basket Ball for Women.* New York: American Sports, 1899.

_____. "Health and Fresh Air." *The Smith College Monthly,* 62-4, 1901.

A Benedictine of Stanbrook Abbey. *Frances Xavier Cabrini: The Saint of the Emigrants.* London: Barnes Oates and Washbourne, 1944.

Blackwell, Elizabeth. *Essays in Medical Sociology,* Vols. I and II. New York: Arno, 1972 (originally published 1902).

_____. *Pioneer Work in Opening the Medical Profession to Women: Autobiographical Sketches.* London: Longmans, Green, 1895.

Bonner, Thomas N. *To the Ends of the Earth: Women's Search for Education in Medicine.* Cambridge, MA: Harvard University Press, 1992.

Borden, Lucille P. *Francesca Cabrini: Without Staff or Scrip.* New York: Macmillan, 1945.

Brady, Terence and Evans Jones. *The Fight Against Slavery.* New York: Norton, 1977.

Burck, Oscar T., Jr., and Nelson M. Manfred. *Since 1900: A History of the United States in Our Times.* 5th ed. New York: Macmillan, 1974.

Cazden, Elizabeth. *Antoinette Brown Blackwell: A Biography.* Old Westbury, NY: The Feminist Press, 1983.

Current Biography. Cori, Gerty T(heresa Radnitz), 135–37, 1947.

Cori, Carl F. "The Call of Science." *Annual Review of Biochemistry.* Vol. 38, 1-20, 1969.

Cori, Gerty T. "Some Thoughts on Science and Society." Panel discussion sponsored by Society of Sigma Xi. Washington University, December 1954 (University of Wisconsin Archives).

Di Donato, Pietro. *Immigrant Saint: The Life of Mother Cabrini.* New York: McGraw-Hill, 1960.

Dykema, Diane J. *Lilly Martin Spencer: Images of 19th Century American Childhood.* Master's thesis. Berkeley, CA: University of California, 1993.

Ellet, Elizabeth Z. *The Women of the American Revolution*, 4th ed. New York: Haskell, 1969 (originally published 1850).

Encyclopedia of World Art. New York: McGraw-Hill, rev. 1968.

Eyman, Scott. *Mary Pickford: America's Sweetheart.* New York: Donald I. Fine, 1990.

Frymir, Alice W. *Basket Ball for Women: How to Coach and Play the Game.* New York: A.S. Barnes, 1928.

Green, J.R. *Medical History for Students.* Springfield, IL: Thomas, 1968.

Greenleaf, Barbara K. *Children Through the Ages: A History of Childhood.* New York: McGraw-Hill, 1978.

Gruver, Rebecca B. *An American History.* Vol. II. Reading, MA: Addison-Wesley, 1972.

Gutman, Herbert G. Entry on Dorothy (Jacobs) Bellanca. *Notable American Women I.* Cambridge, MA: Belknap, 1971.

Hays, Elinor R. *Those Extraordinary Blackwells: The Story of a Journey to a Better World.* New York: Harcourt, Brace and World, 1967.

Helena Rubinstein Foundation. Annual Report. June 1994–May 1996.

Herndon, Booton. *Mary Pickford and Douglas Fairbanks: The Most Popular Couple the World Has Ever Known.* New York: Norton, 1977.

Hill, Naomi E. "Pioneer Women in Physical Education." *Research Quarterly*, 658-65, 1941.

Houssay, Bernardo. Memorial Address. Washington University, December 1957 (University of Wisconsin Archives).

Huber, Peter. "Queen Victoria's Views on Love and Marriage." *Old News*, 11-12, July/August, 1995.

James, Ellen M. Entry on Sophie Irene (Simon) Loeb. *Notable American Women II.* Cambridge, MA: Belknap, 1971.

Keiger, Dale. "The Rise and Demise of the American Orphanage." *Johns Hopkins Magazine*, April 1996.

Kilgore, Kathleen. *Transformations: A History of Boston University.* Boston: Boston University Press, 1991.

Kilpatrick, William H. *Froebel's Kindergarten Principles Critically Examined.* New York: Macmillan, 1916.

Kraditor, Aileen S. *The Ideas of the Woman Suffrage Movement, 1890–1920.* New York: Columbia University Press, 1965.

Kraus-Boelté, Maria and John Kraus. *The Kindergarten Guide.* New York: E. Steiger, 1877.

Lavine, Sigmund A. *Evangeline Booth: Daughter of Salvation.* New York: Dodd, Mead, 1970.

Lawrence, Helen B. and Grace I. Fox. *Basketball for Girls and Women.* New York: McGraw-Hill, 1954.

Lawton, Mary. *Schumann-Heink: The Last of the Titans*. New York: Arno, 1977 (originally published 1928).

Le Gallienne, Eva. *At 33*. New York: Longmans, Green, 1935.

_____. *Flossie and Bessie*. New York: Harper & Brothers, 1949.

_____. *With a Quiet Heart: An Autobiography*. New York: Viking, 1953.

Linkugel, Wil A. and Martha Solomon. *Anna Howard Shaw: Suffrage Orator and Social Reformer*. Westport, CT: Greenwood, 1990.

Loeb, Sophie I. *Epigrams of Eve*. New York: Doran, 1913.

_____. "Johnny Doe, His Mother and the State." *Harper's Weekly*, 24, Jan. 21, 1914.

Lubove, Roy. *The Struggle for Social Security 1900–1935*, 2nd ed. Pittsburgh: University of Pittsburgh Press, 1986.

McGrayne, Sharon B. *Nobel Prize Women in Science: Their Lives, Struggles and Momentous Discoveries*. New York: Carol, 1992.

McHenry, Robert, ed. *Famous American Women: A Biographical Dictionary from Colonial Times to the Present*. New York: Dover, 1983 (originally published in 1980 as *Liberty's Women*).

Mackenzie, Frederic. *The Clash of the Cymbals: The Secret History of Revolt in the Salvation Army*. New York: Bretano's, 1929.

McKenzie, Richard B. "Orphanages: The Real Story." *The Public Interest*, Spring 1996.

McKinley, Edward H. *Marching to Glory: The History of the Salvation Army in the United States of America, 1880–1980*. New York: Harper and Row, 1980.

Marshall, Helen E. *Mary Adelaide Nutting: Pioneer of Modern Nursing*. Baltimore: Johns Hopkins University Press, 1972.

Maynard, Theodore. *Too Small a World: The Life of Francesca Cabrini*. Milwaukee: Bruce, 1945.

The National Cyclopaedia of American Biography XIII. Entries on John Kraus and Maria Kraus-Boelté. New York: James T. White, 1898–1984.

_____. XXIV. Entry on Sophie Irene (Simon) Loeb. New York: James T. White, 1906.

O'Higgins, Patrick. *Madame: An Intimate Biography of Helena Rubinstein*. New York: Viking, 1971.

Palmer, Agnes L. *The Time Between — 1904–1926: Reviewing the Progress of the Salvation Army in the United States Under the Leadership of Commander Evangeline Booth*. Printed by Salvation Army, 1926.

Parascandola, John. Entry on Gerty Theresa Radnitz Cori. *Notable American Women I*. Cambridge, MA: Belknap, 1971.

_____. "Gerty Cori, 1896–1957." *Radcliffe Quarterly*, 11-12, December 1980.

Pickford, Mary. *Sunshine and Shadow*. New York: Doubleday, 1955.

Reynolds, Moira D. *How Pasteur Changed History: The Story of Louis Pasteur and the Pasteur Institute*. Bradenton, FL: McGuinn and McGuire, 1994.

Rothman, David and Sheila M. Rothman. *Sources of the American Social Tradition*. New York: Basic Books, 1975.

Rubinstein, Helena. *My Life for Beauty*. New York: Simon and Schuster, 1964.

Rusk, Robert R. *A History of Infant Education*. London: University of London Press, 1951.

Sandall, Robert. *The History of the Salvation Army*. Vol. I 1865–1878. New York: Nelson, 1947.

Schanke, Robert A. *Shattered Applause: The Lives of Eva Le Gallienne*. Carbondale, IL: Southern Illinois University Press, 1992.

Schumer, Ann Bird. *Lilly Martin Spencer: American Painter of the 19th Century*. Master's Thesis. Columbus: Ohio State University Press, 1959.

Sherr, Lynn. *Failure Is Impossible: Susan B. Anthony in Her Own Words*. New York: Random House, 1995.

Sherwood, Blythe. "She Mothers Many Millions." *National Magazine*, 209+, December 1923.

Sickles, Eleanor M. *Twelve Daughters of Democracy*. New York: Viking, 1941.

Sprigge, Sylvia. *Berenson: A Biography*. Boston: Houghton Mifflin, 1960.

State of New York. *Report of the New York State Commission on Relief for Widowed Mothers*. Albany, NY: J.B. Lyons, 1914.

Stillman, Agnes C.R. *Senda Berenson Abbott: Her Life and Contributions to Smith College and to the Physical Education Program*. Master's Thesis. Northampton, MA: Smith College, 1971.

Sullivan, Mary Louise. *Mother Cabrini: Italian Immigrant of the Century*. New York: Center for Migrations Studies, 1992.

Troutt, Margaret. *The General Was a Lady: The Story of Evangeline Booth*. Nashville, TN: Holman, 1980.

Vargyas, Ellen J. *Breaking Down Barriers: A Legal Guide to Title IX*. Washington, D.C.: National Women's Law Center, 1994.

Victor, Agnes C. *Lone Woman: The Story of Elizabeth Blackwell, the First Woman Doctor*. Boston: Little, Brown, 1970.

Waldon, John D. , comp. *The Harp and the Sword: Writings and Speeches of Evangeline Cory Booth*. Vol. I. West Nyack, NY: Salvation Army Literary Department, 1992.

Walsh, Mary R. *"Doctors Wanted: No Women Need Apply": Sexual Barriers in the Medical Profession, 1835–1975*. New Haven: Yale University Press, 1977.

Webb, Bernice Larson. *The Basketball Man: James Naismith*. Lawrence: The University Press of Kansas, 1973.

Wilson, Philip W. *General Evangeline Booth of the Salvation Army*. New York: Scribner's 1948.

Windeler, Robert. *Sweetheart: The Story of Mary Pickford*. New York: Praeger, 1974.

Zwart, Ann T. Entry on Ernestine Schumann-Heink. *Notable American Women III*. Cambridge, MA: Belknap, 1971.

Index